Fluent in Vietnamese, and a regular visitor to Vietnam, Walter Mason is a brilliant raconteur who gives regular talks and lectures on a wide range of subjects. He has several entertaining blogs including www.waltermason.com, and a strong eye for the quirky.

DESTINATION

Saigon

ADVENTURES IN VIETNAM

WALTER MASON

inspired
LIVING

ALLEN&UNWIN

First published in Australia 2010

Allen & Unwin
83 Alexander Street
Crows Nest NSW 2065
Australia
Phone: (61 2) 8425 0100
Fax: (61 2) 9906 2218
Email: info@allenandunwin.com
Web: www.allenandunwin.com

Cataloguing-in-Publication details available from the National Library of Australia
www.librariesaustralia.nla.gov.au

ISBN 978 1 74175 949 5

Text design by Design By Committee
Typeset by Post Pre-Press Group
Printed by McPherson's Printing Group, Maryborough

10 9 8 7 6 5 4 3 2 1

Mixed Sources
Product group from well-managed forests, and other controlled sources
www.fsc.org Cert no. SGS-COC-004121
© 1996 Forest Stewardship Council
FSC

The paper in this book is FSC certified. FSC promotes environmentally responsible, socially beneficial and economically viable management of the world's forests.

To Ngo Duc Thang, my lifelong companion

CONTENTS

ACKNOWLEDGEMENTS

I'd like to thank my partner, Ngo Duc Thang, for his endless support and patience—without him, nothing would be possible.

I am eternally grateful to my publisher, Maggie Hamilton, a friend and teacher who saw my possibilities.

Many people in Vietnam extended so much kindness and friendship: Kien N, my brother and best friend; the other Kien, who knows who he is; Sister Truth, who tests me and makes demands that strengthen me.

And Thich Nhat Hanh, truly a bodhisattva, whose gentle wisdom has informed my life and spiritual vision for twenty years.

Jan Cornall, one of the great writing teachers and a fascinating person to boot, inspired this book originally.

Finally I'd like to acknowledge Michael Dash and Justine Lee, who have been waiting for this book since 1996, and asking for it constantly. Thanks for your patience and persistence.

INTRODUCTION

I fell in love with Vietnam, because I'd fallen in love. I suppose you could say love followed love. Twenty years ago I met an Australian–Vietnamese man of incredible beauty, grace and good cheer, and he has been my best friend and partner ever since. In 1994 he took me to Vietnam for the first time—I spent my first three days there locked in a room crying, the place terrified me so much. But then something clicked in my psyche. I became obsessed with the place. Since then I have returned again and again.

I've been to Vietnam nine times in all. On one occasion I had three extraordinary months travelling the country with an eccentric Buddhist monk, staying at remote rural monasteries. A decade ago I spent six months studying Vietnamese at the Ho Chi Minh Social Sciences University in Ho Chi Minh City. Most recently I had another three months there while writing the book.

What do I love about the place? The noise, the late-night sounds of karaoke carrying down crowded alleys, and no-one complaining. The crowds that flow and press with such ease. The unabashed curiosity of the people, who are happy to poke me and pull at my body hair and ask me extraordinary personal questions. Whenever I'm there, I'm constantly moved by the great friendliness and kindness of the Vietnamese people.

The sensuousness of the place, the food and the crazy, hot nights linger in the memory, as does the deep vein of mysticism which runs through the country, and is present in every person you meet. There's also the relentless, dizzying speed of change. Things aren't the same from one day to the next. And then, of course, there's the beauty, vivacity, tenacity and charm of the Vietnamese.

There are those things that drive you crazy. The laid-back approach to time. Prepare for a long wait if someone says, 'Oh, about five minutes . . .' The impossibility of walking along the crowded streets, and the occasional accidents; I have fallen and hurt myself badly several times. And also the fact that people will never say 'no', even when they mean it. 'Certainly' means 'maybe', 'probably' means 'probably not', and 'should be ok' means 'not a chance in hell'. It took me a long time to learn this. Then there's the fake monks and nuns who scam tourists in the backpacker districts. And, of course, the heat. I spend an undue amount of time frequenting cafes in an effort to stay out of the sun.

Sometimes it's hard to get beyond the cynicism and sense of hopelessness felt by so many. The system is cruel and corrupt, and holds back the enormous potential of the country. People are poor—so poor that most Westerners simply can't comprehend it. Any gift or tip you give is enormously appreciated and is of great value, helping people to buy some of the basics. It's impossible to avoid beggars and lottery ticket sellers. I always keep a stash of small change in a separate pocket for these people.

The problem is that there's a lot we just don't get. Culturally it's more important to be *seen* to agree than to actually tell the truth. While we may love shorts, I'm afraid they're seen by most Vietnamese as underwear. In Vietnamese culture being wealthy carries with it some real social and familial obligations. The richest person pays, *always*. And you are invariably the richest person. I had to stop kidding myself otherwise, and stop being so damned stingy.

Vietnam offers many gifts. It's given me a more relaxed approach to life, and to spirituality. It's also made me more generous. I now have a much greater sense of myself as someone who has been incredibly fortunate in life, and that I can use my privilege to help others. I have learned to be serene amidst incredible noise and chaos, and I've learned to accept the inevitability of corruption, vanity, avarice and other human failings. I used to imagine that, for example, Buddhist monasteries would be transcendent places of deep spiritual advancement. Instead I discovered they were hotbeds of intrigue, gossip and pettiness, just like everywhere else. In the end it's the everyday moments that captured my imagination, such as the young tradesmen, paint-smeared and laughing, clambering over the ancient statues at a temple in Quy Nhon city as they renovated them in time for the celebration of Amitabha Buddha's feast day. Through all this I've learned to laugh at myself and my hopelessly high expectations.

There's so much of Vietnam that lingers long after I'm home. The memory of hundreds of monks and nuns streaming out of the gates of the Buddhist University on their way home to make the early monastic lunch is something that will never leave me. I cannot forget the colours of their robes, the way their brown, yellow and grey cassocks catch the wind and fly up; their beautiful, smiling faces and the music of their chattering voices. Or the quiet, perfectly proportioned courtyards of Hanoi's Temple of Literature; just being in this ancient shrine to scholasticism is inspiring. Then there was the first time I encountered a street side shrine to Kwan Yin, the Goddess of Mercy, and the first time I ascended those perilously uneven steps to the viewing gallery at the Cao Dai Holy Cathedral, which alerted me to the wonderfully alive mystical sensibility of the Vietnamese people.

Hopefully I am kinder for experiencing all this, more alive to the quieter hopes of human struggle. I don't expect people who are serving me to be super-human any more, and I've learned how to wait. I've learned that shopping and dining and other forms of human interaction can be a divinely subtle dance, simultaneously a flirtation and a test of wills. And there is a wonder in being taken by the hand by a gentle Buddhist monk and led down a quiet country lane to who knows where and just glorying in the magic of the moment. Vietnam is becoming more and more a place of fascination for Western travellers, its beauty and palpable foreignness enormously attractive. My little book is a reflection on the everyday people and the quiet but ever-present rituals that make Vietnam so mysterious, and so intriguing. And being there I was also liberated by the cheerful and frank acknowledgement of my figure flaws. I kind of miss being called fatty, blubber and dumpling by shop assistants, waiters and other people of recent acquaintance.

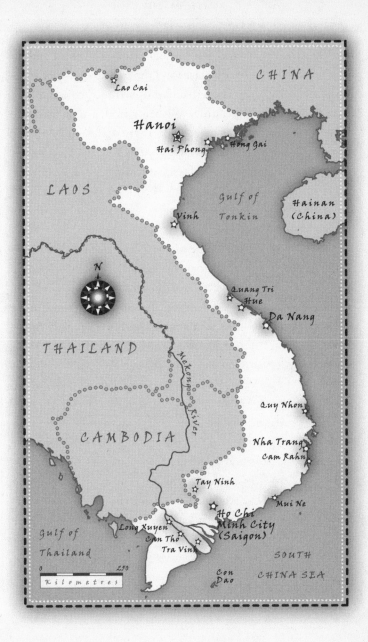

MONKS AND
MOVIE STARS

I came for the vegetarian barbecued pork in the down-at-heel Thuyen Vien restaurant on Nguyen Van Dau street in an un-glamorous suburb of Ho Chi Minh City, once known as Saigon. Served on a tiny little plate, the dish was accompanied by stuffed bitter melons and a sea-salty fungus soup that everyone insisted was very good for me. Like most restaurants in Vietnam, the Thuyen Vien Vegetarian is wildly overstaffed and bursting at the seams with waitresses, plain young country girls who flee in giggles at the sight of a foreigner, and the motorcycle parking area is richly populated by surly, semi-supine youths with cigarette smoke curling from their lips. Though always busy, one has the slightly uneasy feeling that the Thuyen Vien never gets properly cleaned. It is also the kind of place that leaves you worried rather than reassured about the safety of your motorcycle. And the attendants have none of the scrubbed wholesomeness you would expect of the vegetarian.

But, like almost everyone else in the city, we turned up again and again on sabbath nights, joining the amazing throng of mostly young people intent on observing the traditional vegetarian days twice a month. The observance of vegetarianism is an important part of Vietnamese Buddhist culture, though in the easygoing way of Vietnamese Buddhism you only have to do it on certain days. The big sabbath is the fifteenth day of the lunar month, when it is almost impossible to find a seat in a vegetarian restaurant with people queuing out the door in an effort to appear virtuous.

'Don't look now,' hissed Kien, my fashionable young companion, 'but a movie star has just walked in the door—and he's got monks with him!'

Now whenever anyone enjoins me to not look I have an uncontrollable urge to spin around and stare pointedly, which is exactly what I did. I was rewarded with a surprised but dazzling smile. Cosmetic dentistry is very cheap in Vietnam, though generally Western tourists are still wary of taking advantage of it. The movie star was tall, buffed and tattooed, with a luxuriant goatee. His head was shaved, unusual in Vietnam where a bald head is considered the rightful badge of Buddhist monks; to sport one as a layperson is slightly disrespectful. Not that this bothered the two elderly, slightly scruffy monks who accompanied him. They had that cultivated look of nonchalance that universally says: 'Eat my dirt—I'm with someone hot and famous!'

The tall fellow was, my friend assured me, one of Vietnam's

premier movie bad guys. Men blessed with copious body hair were frequently cast as the bad guys in Vietnamese dramas, I'd noticed. Far from playing the villain now, this particular meanie was doing his bit for the faith this sabbath, running back and forth to the alfresco buffet to bring the monks their food.

My friend harrumphed. 'No-one,' he said, 'takes monks out to dinner. This is all for show.' His cynicism was lost on me, however. Always a willing acolyte at the shrine of celebrity, I was ready to be wowed by the villain's good works. He ordered an abstemious bowl of vegetarian noodles for himself, and carefully waited for the monks to begin their meal before he picked up a spoon and started in on the almost tasteless broth. Occasionally he would lean forwards and, using the hand-held end of the chopsticks (the ultimate in self-sacrificing good manners), select a morsel of food to pop into the monks' bowls.

This was too much for my dinner companion. 'Really,' he said, 'there is no need for this. Turning his chopsticks around! In two hours time he'll be sitting down at a goat-meat restaurant!' Spearing a little curried 'prawn' made of tofu skin, he went on, 'Yes, a nice little goat-meat hotpot and a carton of Heineken.'

Glaring spitefully at the movie star's pious table, he added in a hiss, 'And bad girls!'

People are perplexed about why I love Ho Chi Minh City so. They can understand the charm of rural Vietnam, or the quaint antiquity of the northern and central regions, but for most Ho Chi Minh City is a hellish metropolis, a kind of oriental Los

Angeles without the celebrity. It is the kind of place where you can't really cross the road with any sense of security, and where every other person seems to be cultivating some kind of scam that could potentially involve you, the unsuspecting tourist. It is hot and crowded and polluted. And I love it. I love the noisy, laughing people with their delicious food and cheeky manners. I like their brash frankness, their unashamed curiosity and their frequently great kindness, qualities I encountered over and over in Vietnam.

People born and bred there refer to it as 'the City' when they travel. This infuriates those from other cities, particularly Hanoi. Ho Chi Minh City is glamorous, in the way that all big, ugly, congested cities are glamorous. It sucks in all the beauty of the whole country with its promises of riches for girls (and boys) willing to work in entertainment, tourism, hospitality and—inevitably—prostitution. Saigon is full of movie stars, pop stars and restaurant singers who tour the city by night, dropping in at beer halls where they sing a song or two, collect their tips (wrapped elegantly around the stem of a plastic flower) and get back on their bikes to go to their next gig. At the most humble end of the industry are young men from Mekong Delta towns who troll the streetside wine shops with a boom-box attached to a bicycle, singing sad little selections of southern folk music to drunken labourers.

And there are monks—vast quantities of monks. No-one knows how many; no-one keeps count of such things. If other cities seem lacking in monks it is because most of them have set up temporary residence in Saigon in an effort to advance their studies. Like almost everyone else in this crazy city, living is often desperate, and the poorest monks are frequently forced to sing for their supper in the performance of endless funeral duties (for which they are well paid) or temple chores, both of which get in the way of the education they originally came here for.

In 1999 I spent six months studying Vietnamese at the Ho Chi Minh Social Sciences University on Dinh Tien Hoang street in Saigon's District 3. At some point during this period my grandparents, both in their seventies, decided that they'd visit me. My grandma was one of nature's huggers. She adored children, and she loved people in general. Anyone she met who delighted her would be drawn into a hug.

I had explained to her that Buddhist monks weren't really allowed to touch members of the opposite sex, and she seemed to comprehend that restriction. But, a few days after her arrival, when we drove out to a remote village temple in Binh Duong and I introduced her to a gaggle of smiling young monks, she grabbed the one nearest her and drew him into a warm embrace. The other monks, and the old abbott, fell about with laughter as the slender young novice disappeared into my grandmother's ample arms. He returned slightly dazed, but smiling politely.

'Grandma!' I scolded. 'I told you not to touch them.'

'Oh, I know, love, but they're just such sweeties,' she said as she reached for the next one, getting ready to plant a great big kiss on his cheek.

For every monk there are ten nuns, or so it's said. Certainly the city nunneries are bursting at the seams. At the very lowest end, nuns take to the streets morning and afternoon selling humble religious sundries door to door from small baskets. If you ask for a price the tired and sweating young nuns invariably reply, 'Whatever you can offer, brother.'

Visit a temple run by nuns any time just after breakfast and you will see hundreds of grey-robed girls scooting all over the place, smiling shyly and attending to their duties. The inherent sexism of Vietnamese religious culture means that nunneries have traditionally attracted less financial support from lay-people, and so have learned to rely on their own resources and money-making abilities. Ironically, this has seen many nunneries grow more prosperous as the industrious sisters have created profitable industries. Nuns famously own and manage vegetarian restaurants, or produce and distribute the delicious little tofu and gluten dainties that are consumed in vegetarian households across the country. They manufacture Buddhist religious trinkets and ritual objects and distribute religious media such as CDs, books and DVDs. Some of the most delicately fragrant incense in the country hails from small workshops in the courtyards of nunneries, and I have even visited a community of sisters that makes its living from splitting and selling firewood.

Along with its deep spiritual vibe, Ho Chi Minh City displays a mercantile streak that sits proudly with the locals. It is a city full of shopkeepers. The harsh-voiced stallholders at the central Ben Thanh market, with their towering piles of colourful fabric and ambitious prices, serve as the exemplars of Saigon's business spirit, which survived even the harshest dictates of Stalinist-style socialism in the 1980s.

HAIRDRESSERS AND SEAMSTRESSES

The streets of Saigon are filled with businesses, most of them small and many of them serving to support a single family. The people of the south are inveterate shopkeepers, whose very souls were plotting commerce even while the state insisted that private profit was the worst kind of treason.

My old friend and protector in Vietnam, Kien, is of the generation that could launch itself straight into private enterprise. He runs a suburban hairdressing salon in the traditional manner of most Vietnamese bosses: the hours are long, the pay is poor; he is gruff and inclined to bark demands at the employees. But, oddly, the staff are at perfect liberty to disregard almost everything he asks and, despite his crankiness, the stylists and apprentices all seem to adore him. Indeed several of them, male and female, are not-so-secretly in love with him, and will declare to anyone who'll listen that they would die for

Anh Kien. Such devotion, however, does not extend to sweeping up hair when requested, or closing the door to preserve air-conditioning. Sometimes I would question this wilful disobedience, but Kien would merely shrug it off. 'They work long hours,' he reasoned, 'and they don't get paid much.'

'Have you not thought of reducing their hours and increasing their pay? Then perhaps you'd get more out of them.'

Kien snorted at the idea. 'That's just the crazy sort of thing I'd expect a foreigner to suggest. Walter *oi*! You have no understanding of Vietnamese culture.'

Kien is in his early thirties, tall for a Vietnamese of his generation, his face somewhat ravaged by adolescent acne. As befits his trade he is conspicuously fashionable, wearing imported clothes and shoes and driving a new motorcycle that cost more than my small car back home. He tips lavishly wherever we go because, he says, 'People know who I am. I am Kien, the famous hair designer.' He uses the English word 'designer'. He seems at ease with the world, with his foreign friends and casually masculine manner. Women like him—rather too much, as the deterioration of his marriage would attest. He has been my friend, my little brother, my *em trai*, for fifteen years, and I have watched him grow and change along with his country. Both, perhaps, a little friendless.

His has been something of a fairytale Vietnamese life. From picking through rubbish on the mean streets of Saigon's slums, the father of his illegitimate mother returned from overseas in the early nineties and bought the family a house, a business. Almost overnight they were transported from the poorest of the poor to the upper middle classes, but those old memories die hard. Under the fashionable façade Kien is still a tough street kid with a steely heart and a chip on his shoulder a mile wide. Kien is *sad*, and give him a bottle of Heineken or two and he'll tell you so.

His salon sits down one of the many dusty side streets of Ho Chi Minh City, where tourists rarely bother to venture. Such streets are insanely busy, though to the untrained eye it is impossible to distinguish one chaotic alley from another. Men urinate against walls, monks speed by on motorcycles, their brown cassocks floating behind them, and the ubiquitous schoolgirls float along on bicycles, the trains of their elegant white *ao dai* held up on their handlebars. This is the nameless, insignificant part of the city, where people lead everyday lives and work like crazy to establish a place in modern-day Vietnamese urban society.

When Kien and his family care to celebrate a special occasion, they invariably do so at the multi-storied beer restaurant on the corner of Pham Van Hai street. These kinds of mammoth, multi-use restaurants are a stock feature of every suburb in the city. Some floors, designated for family use, are serviced by demure country girls and slouching waiters dressed in crisp black-and-whites with flip-flops. Other floors, however, are for 'businessmen' and the waitresses here are slightly less demure and noticeably more buxom. At closing time these girls frequently leave with the customers. The Vietnamese take a more casual approach to prostitution than do most people in the West. While the fact of prostitution is still borne of poverty and necessity, it is far more prevalent and brazen than many would be used to.

There being no noise regulations in this city, the drunken shouts and toasts from the 'business' floor echo down the street long into the night. The residents, ever respectful of the making of a dollar, never bother to complain.

Kien, too, was a great favourite of my grandparents during their visits to Vietnam. He would take my grandmother to visit the rows of little fabric shops facing the Tan Dinh market in District 3, looking for linens, silks and pure cottons with which to have Chinese blouses made for her. My grandmother would be fussed over by the attendants, all handsome country boys in matching blue gingham shirts.

Then he would take Grandma to our favoured neighbour-hood dressmaker, a quietly spoken woman in an alleyway shop who kept 'traditional' hours—that is, she was almost never open and she took an inordinately long time to make things. But the resultant pieces of clothing were amazing, and amaz-ingly cheap.

While measuring her, the dressmaker would chat endlessly to my grandmother in Vietnamese, calling her 'Honourable Aunt'. My grandmother responded equally merrily in English, each convinced that the other was completely comprehending. She produced the most exquisite blouses for my grandmother, intricately and lovingly stitched, and they remained Grandma's favourite items of clothing until she died.

Every time I returned to Vietnam, Grandma would ask me to give her regards to 'the lovely seamstress', and I always did. I still do, every time having a few shirts made, more out of nostalgia than necessity. Grandma always wore the blouses with a set of prayer beads given to her by her favourite nuns, and she would cut quite an exotic figure at her various parties and outings back at home.

With her new-found cosmopolitanism, my grandmother would often reflect on the strangeness of her destiny, how a woman from small-town Australia could, in her twilight years, have deep and abiding connections in Vietnam, a country that throughout her life had represented a war and little else. She was enormously impressed and affected by the communities of Buddhist monks and nuns she met while she was in Vietnam. When she got back home she called me and asked, 'Is it possible to be a Buddhist and a Christian at the same time?' I assured her that it was, though I warned there were many in both camps who might disagree with us. I sent her a copy of Thich Nhat Hanh's exquisite book *Living Buddha, Living Christ*, and many years later, while she was dying, I discovered it was still one of the books she kept on her side table for daily study.

CONSUMING THE CORPSE FRUIT

In my capacity as cultural bridge, as the unashamed mixer of spiritual traditions, I was viewed as a great source of information by those young monks and nuns enrolled at university. They were hungry for information about the spiritual landscape of the West, and they had heard rumours of the great growth in Buddhism in America and Europe. As unreliable as any information I could convey was likely to be, I was still a living, breathing exemplar of the religious world outside Vietnam. I was often prevailed upon to sing for my supper and act as professional foreigner.

I was scheduled to make one of my movie star–like appearances at the Van Hanh Buddhist University on Nguyen Kie street in the Phu Nhuan district of Ho Chi Minh City. Come 11 am the streets of Phu Nhuan are awash with scores of young monks and nuns returning home to their temples for prayers then lunch. My stints at the university were suggested by Sister Truth, an academic with a doctorate in some arcane facet of ancient Buddhist theology and one of the university's most senior and popular lecturers. My presence in the classes was intended to be purely as observer, but the moment I showed up lectures ground to a halt. I was dragged to the front of the crowded rooms and plonked on a seat as Exhibit A: freaky foreigner who is willing to answer painful questions.

At the end of each excruciating grilling by the energetic young religious I was always bundled away affectionately by old friends. On this day Brother Nguyen took me in hand and suggested we have lunch at a nearby restaurant. Though I was warmed to be walking hand in hand with a gentle young monk, I suspect that some foreigners might be taken aback by the sheer degree of physical affection shown between members of the same sex in Vietnam. It is nothing for a male to take you by the hand while you walk down the street, or to snuggle up next to you in a café and throw an arm over your shoulder.

With a Buddhist university and its legions of monks and nuns, this part of Phu Nhuan district was pretty dense with vegetarian eating places. According to Brother Nguyen, a new one had just opened its doors and it was to-die-for. We eventually came to a swish little house decorated in a quaint country style, hard by a food stall selling barbecued pork sticks emitting a hearty smell of burnt flesh. The irony seemed not to bother my monk, who waved cheerily at the shirtless tough throwing pork across a charcoal grill almost in the vegetarian restaurant's doorway.

As we entered, a lanky, bespectacled and camp young man

came running down the stairs. 'Brothers!' he cried, bringing his palms together at his chest and bowing his head in the charming traditional greeting still observed in religious circles. 'Welcome! So good to see you all! Please come upstairs to our special rooms for monks.'

On our way up he detained me in the stairwell, grabbing me by the arm and addressing me in English. 'You! How are you, sir? Don't I know you from somewhere?' The monks giggled. I broke out into a mild sweat. There were any number of disreputable venues where I could have been observed at play by this queeny maître d'; none of them were places I wanted my religious friends knowing about.

'But of course!' he recalled at last. 'The vegetarian restaurant at Phuoc Hai Temple! I used to be the waiter there—do you remember me?' I didn't, but in my relief I was willing to pledge undying memory and long acquaintance.

As we were ushered into the special monks' suites my heart sank still further. They were a series of banquet rooms kitted out with bamboo mats and dinky little tables standing about thirty centimetres tall. Lunch was served sitting on the floor, with accompanying cramps, backaches and an agonising sensation of pins and needles that wouldn't leave me for days.

Just as I was about to pass out from the pain of my substantial form being packed into the VIP room, the handsome Brother Nguyen called out to the waiters and an enormous tray of durian was brought into the room. The sheer awfulness of durian is legendary, to the point of boredom. The very mention of it causes me to have to stifle a little yawn. 'Ho hum,' I think. 'Repulsive fruit: smells like corpse, tastes like sock—not very interesting. If you don't like it, don't eat it.' But the fact is that until that point I had always managed to politely avoid the eating of durian. It was just one of those standard jokes that helped me play the role of foolish foreigner so well.

'Do you eat fermented prawn paste?'

'No, it stinks.'

'What about durian?'

'No, it stinks.' Cue laughter all round and a communal joy that the Vietnamese can eat almost anything and foreigners are fussy *and* crazy. Everyone satisfied.

Brother Nguyen was so obviously pleased with this special treat that had been organised for me at great difficulty that there was no way I could bow out of it, graciously or otherwise. The fruit was enormous on its platter, a green, spiky hulk that could equally pass as some antique piece of weaponry. As it was being opened and divvied up, its rank smell filling the VIP room forevermore, he expounded at length on how difficult it had been to find such fine fruit out of season.

'I had to travel all over the city,' he smirked proudly. He went into great detail about how much it had cost and how furiously he'd had to bargain with the seller—this kind of commercial minutiae being an essential part of any Vietnamese storytelling. An alarming portion was scooped out onto a plate and handed to me with a flourish. 'A special treat, in honour of our foreign brother.'

Brother Nguyen almost shivered with excitement as the durian was served by the helpful waiters—BYO food never seems to be a problem in Vietnamese restaurants. The largest portion went to me, naturally, and I had nowhere to run.

With his lack of sophistication Brother Nguyen had no idea that foreigners viewed durian with horror, and I couldn't risk offending him and his kindness. I ate manfully—the smell and taste mixing at some mysterious point in my olfactory system so that even holding my breath was pointless.

As I came to the end of my first bowl, almost faint from the effort, the smiling waiters pushed another towards me. Brother Nguyen was pleased with his act of largesse, and made a great show of having the remains of the fruit wrapped in newspaper, 'For you to take home, brother!'

The truth about durian is that, like all truly terrible things, the really awful part is in the preparation and the anticipation. The ghastly appearance of the unopened fruit is so unwelcoming that you wonder how anyone ever thought to open it up in the first place—boredom? Desperation? And then one wonders about the desperate soul who did open it, encountering that sickening stench, and thought, 'Hmmm—anyone for dessert?' Once served up and in one's mouth, the durian sensation is only vaguely unpleasant and more tied up with the eater's previous sensations of disgust. Its flesh (and flesh is decidedly the *mot juste* when one is talking about durian) is remarkably creamy and sweet, a kind of poor man's ice cream.

A durian is a big thing, and the edible parts are handily contained in separate sections within the thorny, deep green outer covering. As there's so much of it, it normally takes a few days to eat. So you regularly encounter a rotting hulk of durian festering half-open on a kitchen bench or dining table in Saigonese homes, everyone seeming quite pleased with the smell. It's a favourite flavouring for cakes and sweets, which is why caution needs to be exercised in selecting sweet deli-cacies so that you don't accidentally bite off a mouthful of, say, a sticky-rice cake only to discover it has been liberally dosed with artificial durian flavour, leaving you feeling anxious and desperate to spit.

TELLING LIES
ABOUT CONFUCIUS

There is a genius for secrecy in the Vietnamese character. People are capable of great mystery, and decades of Communist rule have taught them how best to hide the truth. The seeming rationality of everyday existence is merely a façade, for there is a healthy belief in ghosts and all things psychic that runs deep in the Vietnamese spirit.

While the West relishes TV shows like *Medium*, for the Vietnamese contact with the dead is an altogether more discreet pursuit. As far as I know, spirit possession is still illegal in Vietnam. If any unwary channel were to admit to communicating messages from urgent ghosts of sages past, he or she is likely to find themselves on the wrong side of the law. Yet in spite of this, magicians abound. Hanoi, for all its loveliness, its disintegrating French colonial charm and its recent history of stark Stalinist conformity, is still a city filled with mystics, many of them having long association with the Communist Party. While most tourists are busy planning their side trips to Ha Long Bay, magic is well and truly alive on the grey streets of Vietnam's capital. Perhaps this reflects the richness of the city's history. If you skirt the gorgeous Hoan Kiem Lake late at night you sense the ghosts of its past. Hanoi was for so long a place of unrelenting sadness; its elderly residents all have lost someone near to them. It's no surprise that they should be so eager to make contact with the dead.

While travellers bask in the beauty of the country and the welcome of its people, rarely do they understand the stark realities of the recent past or the restrictions of the present. The people's spirituality is the key to their survival in contemporary Vietnam. It is the one domain in which people can be truly free. The Vietnamese are a resolutely mystical people, and the ideas of Marx and Lenin were always bound to falter among them. There simply is no room for the regime's black and white rules. Everything is negotiated in shifting shades of grey.

Official hostility towards deep spiritual belief is nothing new in East Asia. Confucius, that first great humanist, had mixed feelings about religious fervour. The great irony was, of course, that Confucius' ideas were turned into a quasi-religion, and Confucius the man raised to the rank of folk deity.

It is easy to underestimate the influence of Confucian ideas in Vietnam. The ruling elites followed his system for a millennium and Confucian ideals suffused the educated and aristocratic classes. Phan Boi Chau, the charming poet and gadabout and the grandfather of Vietnamese revolutionary thinking, claimed that he knew Confucius' *Analects* by heart before he was six. Ho Chi Minh's father was an old-style Confucian mandarin, schooled in the Chinese classics and eking out a living as a teacher and regional administrator. With the cult of Ho Chi Minh himself lies the remnants of that Confucian tradition, with Uncle Ho as paterfamilias of a vast, complex family, setting the example of thrift, hard work and devotion to his nation.

One of Hanoi's biggest tourist attractions is Van Mieu, the Temple of Literature. In this medieval Confucian university, Vietnam's brightest once took their exams. It is still a charming place, its hallowed courtyards and gardens haunted by the centuries of scholarship, though its cloisters these days are filled not with the caps and robes of the Confucian mandarin but the ample pastel capri pants of Korean tourists. The gardens are maintained immaculately. When I turned up they were dotted with young, bespectacled students reading *Chicken Soup for the Soul* in Vietnamese.

Though in an otherwise unexceptional quarter of the city, the Temple of Literature stands directly across the road from KOTO, one of the most famous restaurants in Hanoi. Founded by a Vietnamese-Australian, KOTO is staffed entirely by rescued street kids who are trained for a future career in hospitality. The food is delicious and served with aplomb and good grace, but the restaurant has become so popular that you need to get there early to nab a seat. However, a stately morning strolling around the Temple of Literature and a nice early lunch at KOTO make for almost the perfect Hanoi day.

In order to get into the temple complex, the average unattended tourist must run the gauntlet of amateur tour guides who swarm outside the front gates. While waiting in line at the ticket office, I was jostled aside by a slovenly youth in shorts with a cigarette dangling from his lip. He thrust his hand into the booth and demanded four tickets.

Having suffered at the hands of this character, I became curious to see his charges. I was expecting to see a clutch of elderly aunts from some remote village, but instead he passed the tickets out to a group of British tourists. This absolutely intrigued me: how had they fallen for the pitch of this charmless slob in his nylon football shorts and rubber flip-flops? The dress codes of Vietnamese society, while changing in the face of global fashion influences, are still reasonably strict and easily worked out. Tour guiding falls into the semi-respectable realm of satellite white-collar work, and so requires its practitioners to be dressed smartly and professionally. Such things are taken seriously in Vietnam, particularly in the more conservative north. This ingénue was blatantly flouting all conventions, and so I decided to tag along at a respectful distance and trail his tubby form throughout the temple complex.

He kept a lighted cigarette about his person for the duration of the tour—including inside the ancient wooden halls and shrine rooms. His English was remarkably good, though his frowning face and barking voice did little to endear him. As I listened more carefully to his spiel, I suddenly realised that all his dates, names and explanations of architecture and statuary were spectacularly wrong, a mishmash of myth, misplaced history and sheer invention. He was just making it up as he went along. The elderly tourists were intrigued by his stories.

When they arrived at the main shrine to Confucius, who

had never set foot in Vietnam, he began telling them a long and involved story about how the Great Sage had constructed the temple and graduated the first scholars. As the tour closed, the bare-faced fantasist had the hide to affect a look of woundedness when he received his tip from the tourists. He held his lies in such high esteem that he had obviously hoped for more.

JASPER PRAYER
BEADS

For those used to the overt religiosity of the south, downtown Hanoi can seem remarkably denuded of religious buildings. While traversing the Old Quarter one rarely sees monks, and most of the temples you visit have the suspicious air of over-preservation, of careful attention to history but an absence of living devotion. The exception is the Ambassadors' Pagoda, which serves as the main functioning Buddhist temple in central Hanoi.

The Ambassadors' Pagoda is beautifully placed on Quan Su street, one of Hanoi's grand boulevards. These wide, tree-lined streets are crypto-Parisian fantasies that were much beloved by the colonial planners. To walk to the Pagoda from Hoan Kiem Lake you need to pass Hanoi Cathedral, a stark, grey and faux-gothic structure permanently streaked with bird shit, whose forlornness cannot be lightened by the latest hideous banner strung up across its façade. The whole banner-on-religious-buildings situation has only been worsened by the accessibility of design software and the cheapness of printing technology. Catholics are particularly prone to these sins against aesthetics, festooning exquisite stone exteriors with canary yellow vinyl posters urging the world to remember some terrible situation or forgive some injustice. Hanoi Cathedral is such a forbiddingly austere edifice that it seemed almost to swallow the offending five-metre high banner. For some reason the cathedral seems never to be open; I have been to Hanoi many times and never once have I seen the inside.

The Ambassadors' Pagoda, so named because in the fifteenth century it was the official residence for foreign visitors to the city, is a squat yellow building with a tree-filled courtyard. On sabbath afternoons the street outside the temple is crowded with elderly women selling religious paraphernalia from hand-woven baskets. Cheap wooden rosaries, little machines that chime the Goddess of Mercy's name in a perpetual loop and tiny red envelopes filled with reprints of the *Lotus Sutra* are all popular items. I always try to frequent these stalls because the women themselves are such characters, with their betel-stained teeth and unending tales of woe. The temple itself also has a shop, with the typical assortment of religious clothing and bronze bells. I was in the shop examining a beautiful set of jasper prayer beads when I felt a tug on my elbow and looked down into the plump face of a Hanoi schoolboy.

'Big Brother,' he lisped, 'I am delighted that you are a fellow Buddhist. This shop is so rich in the Dharma! Why, I was just considering purchasing these DVDs.' And he thrust out a fist full of video recordings of famous monks' lectures, a staple offering of temple shops throughout the country. Amused by this precocious ten-year-old boy, I said magnanimously, 'Let me buy them for you, Little One.'

'What a good man!' he exclaimed, while a curious audience built up around us. The woman behind the counter smelled blood and selected a half-dozen more DVDs for my little friend. When I warily agreed to these extra purchases, he casually threw a couple of books and a cheap plastic rosary into the bundle. I handed over the beautiful jasper prayer beads to be wrapped and asked for the bill.

'Such a fine person,' said the old lady behind the counter. 'Being so generous to a little Buddhist!'

I paid her and she carefully wrapped all my purchases up and popped them into a single bag, which she handed over to the little boy, my expensive jasper beads and all.

'Oh, but . . .' I began. Little Buddha had already plunged his dirty hands into the bag and torn the wrapping from the jasper beads. Throwing them over his head with a triumphant smirk, he said, 'And these, Big Brother, I will wear every time I pray, and I'll think of you.'

A more assertive person would have snatched the jewellery straight out of the hands of this greedy little busybody, but I just didn't have the guts to say, 'Gimme back my beads, peewee.'

'To repay you for your kindness, let me show you around the temple,' he said. I felt I should try to get my money's worth from the little extortionist, and I am kind of glad I did. He took me up stairs and through doors and into shrines I just hadn't known existed, despite having visited the temple on numerous occasions. At each shrine, the pint-sized bodhisat-tva made an elaborate obeisance to the deity, showing off to anyone who might be looking.

When the tour ended we took a seat in the temple garden and my guide piped up, apropos of nothing, 'Boy, I'm hungry. Aren't you hungry?'

'No, I've just eaten, actually.'

'Not me—I haven't had a bite since morning. I'm hungry enough to die. I could just murder a couple of deep-fried bananas.'

There he sat, absolutely brazen on the concrete temple seats, my twenty-dollar jaspers around his neck, expecting me to shell out some cash for his afternoon snack.

'No, really,' I demurred, 'I couldn't eat another thing.' I wasn't about to fall for his little scam.

'But surely,' he said, his little mouth crumpling, 'kind Big Brother can give a child 5000 dong to buy some bananas?'

'Okay,' I agreed, pulling out my wallet, but shaking my head to let him know I understood he was making a fool of me.

'Make it 10,000,' he said sharply, 'and I'll bring some back for you.'

Left alone at last, I strolled around the temple. There was another shop, hidden in the cloisters and operated by a quiet, beautiful young woman reading, you guessed it, *Chicken Soup for the Soul*. She was one of those disinterested sales people who always turn me into a rampaging consumer. Everything was quite cheap, so I bought Buddha pendants and cinnamon-scented incense, and copies of all the latest Buddhist magazines and journals, though I never had any hope of understanding the stories inside. I just knew that if I were Vietnamese, I would be buying these magazines. It was my way of creating a new self in this alien place. The separation from the written word while living in a foreign country is often hard to bear. Language shapes us and gives people all sorts of clues about who we are. The only way I can attempt this in Vietnam is to haunt the temple bookshops and buy cheap religious magazines, scanning them for familiar words and staring at the pictures for inordinately long periods of time.

Back in the courtyard with my bag full of purchases I saw my little guide, his grimy hands popping the very last banana fritter into his mouth.

'Heavens!' he slurred, rolling his eyes in an exasperated mime. 'I thought you must have gone. I'm afraid I had to eat all of the bananas.'

'It doesn't matter, I'm going home now.'

'Going home? How are you getting home?'

'Walking.'

'Walking! If only I had that luxury. I'm afraid it's a long bus ride for me.'

'Well, have a safe journey.'

'The really sad thing is, Big Brother, I don't have the money for a bus fare.'

Not speaking, I reached into my wallet and handed him a 10,000 dong note.

'Make it twenty,' he said, 'and I can buy some fruit for my grandmother.'

LATIN QUARTER

It is often difficult to drive a taxi into Hanoi's 'Latin Quarter', a dogleg of cafés, pubs and restaurants a brief moment's walk from Hoan Kiem Lake. On this occasion I didn't bother, largely because the taxi driver, in fine old Hanoi tradition, had already turned a five-minute trip into a fifteen-minute one. I begrudged forking out more ill-gotten dong due to his dodgy meter. Besides, I've seen taxi drivers hit motorcycles that are quadruple parked on the corner of this busy little section, and I didn't fancy a conflict with the irate hoodlum who would inevitably emerge screaming from one of the bars. So I walked up the street and into a smoky, dimly lit little coffee shop on Hang Hanh street and perched precariously on one of the ubiquitous plastic chairs.

I have learned to treat Vietnamese plastic furniture with a great deal of care. More than once my substantial form has caused the collapse of seemingly sturdy moulded plastic seating, to the great delight—and occasional fear—of the people sitting nearby. Once a group of friends took me to a rabbit-meat restaurant and, well-lubricated with cheap Vietnamese beer, I was laughing and gesticulating and otherwise bouncing in my little plastic seat. The back legs began to sink, first slowly and terribly, and then buckling completely, sending me flying backwards. I tumbled straight into the restaurant's shrine, leaving myself covered with incense ashes, cold tea and squashed bananas. As I was falling, my legs flipped our table over and a perfectly good meal of barbecued rabbit was tossed across the restaurant floor. This was all treated with a great deal of laughter and good cheer, and everything was soon put to rights. I was presented with two plastic chairs, one slid on top of the other, an excellent, and safe, solution.

Back in the café on Hang Hanh street, I was surrounded by chain-smoking ruffians and coarse-voiced Hanoi hookers. Squashed into my plastic chair I took on an almost zen-like stillness, trying to take most of my weight on my legs and thighs, in effect squatting more than sitting. The whole effort was exhausting. A bored-looking waiter, smoking a cigarette, came over to take my order. Foreigners are not uncommon in the Latin Quarter, and he was decidedly unimpressed. 'What do you want?' he asked in English.

'One glass of hot milk coffee, please,' I responded in my best Saigon accent.

'*Troi oi!* What have we got here? "*Hot milk coffee*",' he minced, making fun of my accent, and glancing around to the various gangsters in the surrounding tables, drawing them into the joke. 'Just a minute now—where did you learn to speak like that, Big Sister?' The café gang all laughed at this aspersion. 'You can't be speaking like that around here! You sound like a little Saigon tart. "*Hot milk coffee!*" For a start, in Hanoi men don't take milk in their coffee.'

When the waiter eventually plonked my order down on the shaky table, he said, 'Here's your coffee, Little One,' and once more brought down the house.

The next morning, very early, I was strolling past the café and the same insolent waiter was there, stretched out across three motorcycles, smoking. Noticing me walk by, he raised himself up on his elbow and extravagantly gestured into the café with his other hand.

'Come in for a coffee, Fatty,' he invited.

Hanoi boasts of one or two very good, expensive French restaurants. The French come to Vietnam, one supposes, in the spirit of nostalgia, hoping to revisit the scenes of their ancestors' follies and to glory in the crumbling decadence that recalls the spirit of Pierre Louÿs, Marguerite Duras and, on a good day, Catherine Deneuve in *Indochine*. The remnants of French cuisine are in evidence: the ubiquity of good coffee and big baskets of baguettes sold on street corners. If you search a restaurant menu carefully enough you will discover the Vietnamese still eat ragout and frogs' legs fried in butter. But to most the French era is now the stuff of fairytale, too much in the distant past to seem significant. Only the very old speak any French.

In fact the French colonial period seems merely to be a mystery to the vast numbers of young Vietnamese born since 1975. It is simply not a part of their cultural consideration. There is neither a painful recollection of colonial shame nor a romantic nostalgia for a French past. There is, instead, an obsessive concern with Vietnam's future, and with the realities of getting by today. Any French colonial history that lingers seems to exist mostly for tourists and for those dwindling members of the Communist Party who have a vested interest in banging on about the horrors of the past.

But Hanoi still manages to flirt with Francophile elegance, with its tiled cafés and little bistros tucked up elegant stairways on Ngo Bao Khanh street. The Mocha Café on Nha Tho street still carries a collection of pirated French paperbacks, though they look a little dusty. France is still palpable in Hanoi, which is why the tourists tend to love it so. The melancholy, too, of the average resident in Hanoi is vaguely Gallic, though I suspect it is equally a part of traditional Vietnamese culture.

It doesn't help that after 1975 the new independent government did all it could to eradicate the memories of the past, mostly through the distinctly Confucian method of renaming things. Given their way, the ideologues of the Socialist Republic of Vietnam would have bulldozed the glorious French colonial buildings and erected en masse the brutalist cement boxes that characterise communist architecture everywhere. But poverty and necessity, those handmaidens of fate, intervened, and the old buildings were made to serve a new purpose. Not so the old names, which were jettisoned in order to create a new social narrative.

Socialist governments the world over have erased so much of the past, including the words and language of old regimes. Vietnam has had more than its share of this treatment, especially in Ho Chi Minh City—nee Saigon. Once romantic streets and boulevards have now been renamed in honour of obscure moments in Vietnamese revolutionary history. Sadly these less than inspired names seem to have stuck. But try as they might, the government can never get anyone from District 3 inward to call Ho Chi Minh City anything but Saigon.

Indeed, it is in Hanoi where the use of the name 'Saigon' seems most prevalent. For those in the West who have studied the Vietnam War (known in Vietnam as the American War), there is a heavy investment in the idea that the north and south of Vietnam are basically the same. But spend any time in Vietnam and you will see that the regional differences in this long, narrow country are deep and significant. There is a vast lingual, cultural and historical rift between north and south that most foreigners underestimate.

At least in Hanoi the Saigonese are admired and viewed as exotic and fun, but sadly this admiration seems only to work one way. In Saigon northerners are still largely despised, making up as they do a massive underclass of menial labourers and service workers. People in Ho Chi Minh City still speak of 'my difficult cousins', a derogatory term for northerners. A standard joke is to say, 'Make yourself at home—just like a northerner would.' I have been terribly embarrassed when northern friends have visited me in the city and been subjected to dismissive service and pained expressions in restaurants and shops, as though their very words were an agony for delicate Saigonese ears.

But in the Frenchified cafés that line the shores of Hanoi's Lake Hoan Kiem, it can be equally difficult for southerners to negotiate an order when simple linguistic differences are suddenly thrown into relief. For all their elegance, Hanoian waitresses are noted for their sangfroid, and it doesn't take much for them to dismiss a customer entirely. As I sat on the terrace of a lakeside café for the first time my beautiful waitress simply walked away after I used the southern words for 'cup', 'pineapple' and 'iced coffee'. Clad in a tight, silky, plum-coloured *ao dai*, the provocative national costume of Vietnam, she threw up her hands in mock exasperation to the gaggle of staff sitting bored at the other end of the café. 'Would someone else serve that foreigner?' she demanded. 'I can't understand a word he says.'

MYSTICAL HANOI

My friend Khoa had the face of a mystic. I'd known him back home, one of the new breed of Vietnamese students sent to study in the West. Children of Communist Party scions and army bigwigs, they were a new privileged class that had absorbed the ideas of Marx and Lenin at the teat and were subsequently sent to Sydney, Texas or Montreal to study business, marketing and economics. While a student Khoa had been rebellious, dying his hair blond and cultivating an interest in feng shui and the I Ching. But on his return to Vietnam he had been re-absorbed into his impeccably revolutionary family, married off and ushered into a sensible job. When I caught up with him at the Polite Pub on Pho Bao Khanh, Khoa could have passed for any other Hanoi resident in his early thirties, dressed sensibly, bordering on unfashionably. He also smoked cigarette after cigarette. No longer the fresh young thing I had known in what were doubtlessly more carefree student days, he still had the same beautiful, high-cheekboned face and haunted, poetic eyes. He still ached for something greater and was, at heart, still a mystic.

I was excited to be out on the town in the cool Hanoi night. There really is something special about Hanoi at night, walking its quiet, ill-lit streets in the shadows of crumbling colonial façades evoking a down-at-heel splendour. It is filled with young people, but their personalities, too, are hemmed in by all the history. It's always been hard to be a free spirit in Hanoi.

'The thing is,' said Khoa, 'my work bores me. I never wanted to be an analyst for a construction firm! I keep cutting back days at the company and my family gets angry at me. But it's now or never—I need to follow my heart.'

Khoa and a group of his friends had opened up a small office out by the West Lake where they gave feng shui readings and cast the I Ching for interested clients. Feng shui really has experienced a huge resurgence in interest in Vietnam; little neighbourhood feng shui shops have sprung up all over the country. The feng shui wizard is nothing new, and was always an integral part of traditional village life. This new breed of practitioner is merely an urbanised, modernised rendering of a more ancient memory.

I was surprised to discover they were doing a roaring business, especially Khoa with his computerised forecasts using software he'd bought overseas. The construction company functionary was moonlighting as a soothsayer, and his loyalties were torn.

'Take a look at this,' said Khoa, pulling a scroll of thick rice paper out of his bag. When he unrolled it I saw it was covered with the most exquisite calligraphy. Assuming it to be Chinese, I examined it more carefully and discovered it wasn't.

'But what language is it?' I asked. 'It might be Chinese, but it's not. Is it Tibetan? Sanskrit? Some kind of Khmer . . . ?'

'Ah,' said Khoa, blowing smoke out of his nose and throwing back a mouthful of Heineken. The Polite Pub was filling with yuppies and tipsy Western girls, and people were casting glances at us and our unlikely scroll of hieroglyphs. 'This is the language of the underworld!' Khoa looked proudly at the paper. 'This is my own calligraphy. I have been studying it for years now with a special master—I cannot tell you his name—but he has travelled to the other realms and has studied the language used by the Kings of Hell . . . and others. Angels, Buddhas . . . On the other side, this is the language of administration. I am only just beginning to master it.'

Given Khoa's unwillingness to serve in an administrative position in this life I did wonder why he felt the need to study the nitty-gritty of the clerical classes beyond the veil, but I didn't question him on this. 'Can I meet the Master?' I asked.

'Oh no—we need to be discreet. We still need to be careful about such things in Vietnam.' This was a great admission from Khoa, who was an avid believer in the Vietnamese socialist state. 'Things will change,' he assured me. 'Things will get better as the generation shifts. Even Party members now are interested in spirituality.'

This was something I was to hear again and again. The staunchest Party members were all growing old, and the world was changing very quickly. They now had questions that couldn't be answered by the philosophies of Marxist dialectical materialism. Party members were beginning to visit temples and monks, I was assured. Even mediums and fortune tellers were beginning to gain a following among the upper echelons of the socialist ruling elite.

In Hanoi there was one particular medium, a middle-aged woman, who enjoyed a great deal of patronage from the army elite and other members of the ruling classes. She had risen to fame by falling into trances and correctly identifying the locations of the remains of missing soldiers lost during the long war. Parents who had buried their grief for decades began to frequent her séances. Like all bereft parents, they were hoping for news of their long-lost children. The long war took a terrible toll on the families of the North, and so many children were lost, though never forgotten. For thirty years the Vietnamese government has managed to keep this sort of thing tucked away and illegal, but it seemed that the tide was turning. Perhaps the spirits of the dead did want to make themselves known. Certainly the long-buried grief of mothers, who were only ever consoled by the idea that their children had died for independence and socialist perfection, has come bubbling to the surface in their twilight years. This medium, I heard, had opened up a chain of successful vegetarian restaurants in Hanoi—more evidence that old ideas were beginning to resurface in the northern capital that had once prided itself on its destruction of supernatural silliness.

Khoa was concerned that I had been offended by his refusal to introduce his Master. 'But you can come to the office tomorrow,' he promised, grasping my arm warmly.

'Come and see the feng shui masters at work. You will be good luck for us.'

Never one to miss a colourful experience, I readily agreed.

The next day it was raining. Not just the usual Hanoi rain, but torrential sheets that splashed back up out of the filthy gutters onto your clothes and face. Hanoi had just suffered a spate of floods and I had been advised not to visit the city at this time. Never one to let popular forecasts cramp my plans, I had blithely waved away the concerns of friends in Ho Chi Minh City who had clipped out newspaper images of cars and houses swept away by flash flooding in the Hanoi suburbs. I was often dismissive of media coverage of 'disasters'; now I was beginning to wonder if they hadn't actually been right.

In my hotel lobby I peered out the glass doors. The rain was so heavy that the morning was as black as night, and visibility almost nil. But right on 7 am, the time we had arranged to meet, Khoa called me on my mobile. 'Shall I come and pick you up?' he asked.

'Have you not seen the weather outside? I hardly think you could handle my weight on the back of your motorcycle in this rain. We would both be killed,' I responded, saying I'd make my own way there.

Reluctantly I stumbled out into the weather searching for a taxi, which was surprisingly easy to find. It took me on the usual circuitous route to the West Lake, then dropped me off outside a little shopfront attached to an enormous blue villa.

Its metal grille was locked tight against the wind and rain. In front was a sign advertising it as the Society for the Study of Feng Shui in the East. There was no awning under which to wait, so I stepped out into the street and the driving rain to seek out some shelter.

Almost immediately I felt the terrible shock of being hit by something travelling at speed, and my body swung round. Miraculously I managed not to fall. The little old lady who had hit me was wearing a straw conical hat, and was madly trying to stop her bicycle using only her feet and rubber flip-flops.

'Heavens!' she called, dismounting from the bicycle and rushing back towards me. 'Are you all right, Little Brother?'

I smiled and shrugged, though in truth my head and heart were pounding from the shock, and my left shoulder and ribs were already throbbing with pain.

'Lord! I thought I'd killed you,' she said as she took off her hat and held it over me in a kindly gesture. 'What are you doing out in this rain, sir? Don't you know you could be washed away in a flood? Stay indoors!' she admonished as she went to pick up her bike. 'My old bike's got no brakes, and I've no money to fix it. Are you sure you're okay?' Then she leapt back up onto her bike and began to coast once more down the hill, headed who knows where in the midst of a typhoon.

Through the interminable rain I limped to a nearby awning. Nothing was open. No-one was around. After some time Khoa pulled up, blissfully unapologetic about his lateness. He opened the shop and, in spite of the deluge, it soon filled with various mediums, clairvoyants and feng shui wizards, all in a gloomy frame of mind because inclement weather meant customers would be pretty thin on the ground. I asked a pudgy-faced woman, an expert in the I Ching, what were the main problems clients brought to her. 'Oh, that's easy,' she said. '*Is my husband having an affair?* Followed by: *Will my husband come back to me?* And the third most popular is: *Should I leave my husband?*' This drew chuckles from the other seers, all of whom agreed that this was, indeed, the bulk of their business dealings.

By midday, not a single paying customer had crossed the threshold. The pudgy-faced lady suggested that my presence might be to blame for the downturn in business. Knowing that my invitation may have been outstayed, and nursing an aching butt from hours sitting on a tiny blue plastic stool, I announced my departure. Khoa took me back out into the maelstrom to find a taxi, and bizarrely the whole little hilly street was lined with them. Each one had a driver inside stretched out across the back seat, sound asleep. We knocked on the window of one or two, but the drivers kept sleeping. One looked up groggily and waved us away in annoyance. Finally we managed to rouse a gruff-voiced fellow, who agreed to take me back to my hotel.

'There are floods, you know,' he said, shaking his head sadly. 'Driving around on the streets is very dangerous. I can get you back home, but I'm afraid we'll have to take a round-about route.'

I slumped down into my seat, my whole body aching from the morning's collision and beginning to feel feverish.

'Just drive,' I said.

WHEN CHEAP
ISN'T CHEERFUL

I f you are ever looking for a hotel in Hanoi, I recommend you check the room before you agree to the tariff. Rooms with windows can be rare in the city, so it is easy to disappear into a black hole with no circulation and ample damp and quite possibly fall asleep for days, waiting for a dawn. I had been careful to find a room in the cheery little Kim Hoang Gia Hotel with a balcony, overlooking a noisy restaurant and a *tam quat,* an all-male massage house that employs blind masseurs. For a foreigner, getting a legitimate massage in Vietnam can be quite a difficult thing, and I had heard horror stories of notorious goings-on even in five-star hotel spas. So I studiously avoided the *tam quat*, and as a result the touts outside made rude comments to and about me whenever I entered or left my hotel. But that was the lesser of two evils, as far as I was concerned.

The streets of Hanoi's Old Quarter are filled with picturesque cyclos and less romantic taxis; almost all are entirely untrustworthy, and the witless tourist is still considered fair game. The cyclos will take you on a brief spin through Hanoi's crowded streets and smilingly steal you blind at the end of it, feigning confusion about numbers or currencies. Go for a ride on a cyclo by all means, but negotiate a price beforehand and ensure that you have said 'Vietnam dong'. It's a common scam to agree on a price and then at the end of it have the driver say, 'No, I meant US dollars!' Don't accept any detours. If they offer you a ridiculously low price for a ride, don't take it. They will whisk you straight to some awkward scam that will take you an hour to extract yourself from. It is all a part of the Hanoi experience. Becoming upset about it is entirely useless.

Still bruised and sore from the morning's accident, coming down from my room for dinner I stepped out of the lift and heard a terrible crack, followed by the sensation of sinking, then falling into a hole of my own creation. This caused an enormous fuss and a great deal of gabbling by the hotel staff. It seemed that the tile directly in front of the lift had been covering an enormous hole, and my weight had caused it to crumble. Fortunately I hadn't hurt myself, though my pride was wounded by having a whole lobby full of people witness my inelegant collapse. As staff made a fuss, in truth I was close to tears. This was, after all, my second major accident of the day. All I could think was, 'They are going to charge me for this. I am going to have to pay for this stupid fucking tile.'

You see, I have something of a history of breaking things in Vietnam, firstly due to the fact that I am a large man and take up the space of at least three Vietnamese people. Everything in Vietnam, naturally enough, is built to Vietnamese scale and, unlike at home, the world is simply not created for my easy passage. The second major reason is that, almost without exception, everything in Vietnam is manufactured, assembled and constructed shoddily and cheaply. Anyone who's ever bought anything in Vietnam, particularly something with a practical application, will attest to this.

This jerry-built quality has a significant psychological effect on the Vietnamese people. On the one hand, they treat everyday objects with a remarkable lack of care. At Kien's hairdressing salon, the apprentices casually toss CDs onto benches and on top of the CD player, never returning them to their protective cover. As a result, CDs rarely lasted longer than a week or two. This carelessness used to drive me crazy. One day I mentioned it to Kien. He simply shrugged and said, 'It doesn't matter. Vietnamese CDs stop working quickly anyway. Why take care of them?'

I declared this was an appalling state of affairs and, wanting to set an example, I bought some new CDs and proceeded to treat them with exaggerated care, always replacing them in their sleeves as soon as they were finished. Sure enough, after about ten days the CDs stopped working, exactly like the ones the apprentices used as drink coasters. This constant disintegration of things is enormously depressing after a while, and does encourage a contemptuous view of material objects. On the other hand, if they can possibly afford it the Vietnamese will spend an inordinate amount of money on buying superior, imported products. My quest for bargains simply bewildered people. 'If I had the money to buy something good, I certainly would,' they said. 'But you, you seem to go out of your way to buy rubbish.'

Caveat emptor is almost a religion in Vietnam and if, like me, you go around breaking things, you should expect to pay for them. Once, for example, in a froufrou café in Ho Chi Minh City, I brushed against a cabinet that wobbled insecurely on a sunken tiled floor. A small vase of truly phenomenal ugliness came crashing to the ground, showering me with little fuchsia-coloured shards of glass. Later when I called for the bill, it listed, along with my coffees: 'Broken vase—50,000 dong.'

So I squatted, sad and sore and humiliated, on a moderately priced hotel floor, plunged into a depression quite specific to Hanoi, and already angry that I would almost certainly face the injustice of having to pay for this in several days' time when I had to settle the bill. It's worth noting here that I was never actually charged for the broken tile, which speaks volumes for the hotel and its management. Throughout the rest of my stay, however, the tile was never repaired. Someone, probably one of the jolly young doormen who chased the *tam quat* touts away from me, simply threw an ingenious rubber mat across the hole, thereby rendering it invisible and horribly dangerous. I learned to step across it each time I exited the lift, but I can't help but worry that somewhere is an unsuspecting tourist who came to grief by stumbling into this rubber-covered hole. And it was all my fault.

Hanoi is inclined to be cold and grey, especially during a serious monsoon. The streetscapes usually shifted magically from morning to afternoon to evening as different vendors enjoyed their share of passing trade; a pavement tea stall suddenly opening here, an ancient woman throwing down a cloth and selling fresh bunches of coriander there. But in the rain they all disappeared, opting no doubt to stay in for the day while the streets were left to soak in solitude.

Like many old cities, Hanoi is a cramped place. Its long, narrow houses face each other across narrow, ancient streets that are no more than glorified alleys. I had shelled out for a room with a balcony and, despite the rain and the freezing weather, I was determined to make the most of my little piece of sunshine. Somehow, along with a massive air-conditioning unit and a selection of bonsai and other potted plants, they'd managed to squeeze an iron table and chair onto the balcony, so I sat out there in the howling wind writing up my journal.

My balcony looked directly on to the beer garden of a busy restaurant across the street. So close did the two levels seem that it was surely possible for a person to reach out from each side and touch hands. The restaurant was notable for its incredible noise which went well into the night, its clusters of office-worker patrons getting progressively drunker and egging each other on with more and more voluble group toasts. But on this rainy and windy afternoon the street was deserted, and the beer garden was forlornly empty. A young waiter and waitress sat bored at a table, talking quietly, completely oblivious to my presence just across the narrow street. Within moments they were pressed close together, then kissing passionately and, they thought, invisibly.

I wondered if I should cough, or move my iron chair across the balcony tiles to announce myself. But soon it was too late. If they glanced up now I looked like a shame-faced old voyeur. As clothing was dislodged and hands moved into parts invisible, I quietly stood up and went back to my room. Then, discreetly lowering my plantation shutters on the amorous couple, I silently wished them the best, pleased they were making the most of an otherwise wasted afternoon.

Such public love-making is common in overcrowded Vietnam. A propped-up motorcycle parked on the side of a dark road frequently serves as an alfresco boudoir for poverty-stricken young lovers. Cinemas and darkened cafés are also commonly used trysting places, and the only honourable thing to do when confronted with such couples is to discreetly avert the eyes, though I don't think for a minute this is what usually happens.

But, alone in my hotel room, I was plunged into the cold, grey depression that is common to those stuck in a foreign city in bad weather. I reflected on how far Hanoi had come since 1994 when I first visited it. Poor old Uncle Ho, now preserved in great state in his monumental mausoleum across the city, had visions of a different world. What would he have made of all this? Copulating youngsters in advertising-emblazoned beer gardens and idle foreigners in boutique hotels. Was this the socialist paradise of which he'd dreamed? I suspect not.

THE TOWERS
OF BINH DINH

While Vietnamese life changes rapidly, the Buddhist world continues to go on more or less as it has for centuries. Particularly in regional areas, there is a carefully preserved world of monastic institutions that are filled with kind and colourful characters. They too are young, but in their youth they are bound to ancient traditions that see them, ironically, the arbiters of old ways. My friend Thay Chau, only thirty-eight, was already the abbott of a busy temple in Quy Nhon city.

Thay Chau's office is a little disorganised. Being the workplace of a moderately busy Buddhist abbott, it is packed full of wooden Chinese-style furniture that is rather impressive as furniture goes, solid and dark. I always felt comforted when I saw it, restful in the guarantee that here was a chair that would not crumble under my weight. The substantial seats were capacious enough to allow a monk to fold his legs up in the lotus position and sit comfortably for hours, chatting and smoking and eating watermelon seeds with anyone who might drop by.

The glass-topped coffee table was slick with spilled tea and there was an overflowing ashtray being regularly contributed to by the abbott himself. Though smoking is less and less popular among monks, Thay Chau told me that, unfortunately, he was forced to maintain the terrible habit. 'My asthma, you see,' he explained dolefully, reaching for a bottle of green liniment to further underline his predicament.

Indeed, Abbott Chau's health did seem to be perilous. He was plump, or would be plump were he twenty or thirty centimetres taller. As it was, he was a short man and his plumpness was elevated somewhat to fatness. He suffered from sleep apnoea, and his thunderous snores could be heard throughout the temple complex at night. This same affliction also left him with terrible headaches and a generally dozy character. It was nothing for Abbott Chau to drop off to sleep while sitting in the midst of a chattering group of guests, or during evening prayers. It's fair to say that Abbott Chau was not exactly the most energetic character, and he was somewhat inclined to indulge the large community of young monks of which he had charge. He was far too genial a man to be an effective disciplinarian.

His roly-poly form and his fat, smiling face did, however, make him an extraordinarily popular figure in his community, and monks from far and wide (and there are a lot of monks in Binh Dinh province) came to visit him and pay their respects every day. The messy abbott's room, with its piles of unattended papers and boxes of gifts and offerings pushed into its corners, was constantly busy, and Thay was the consummate host, rarely budging from his wide, hard chair in the corner.

Despite being the capital city of Binh Dinh province, Quy Nhon remains a rather pretty but very neglected part of the central Vietnamese coast. Nobody comes here, and there seems little reason to. There is a busy working port, some small but lovely beaches, and a fascinating collection of ancient religious towers built by the indigenous Cham people. Binh Dinh is also famous throughout Vietnam for its martial artists and its monks. But none of these attractions seem sufficient to lure tourists in any significant numbers, despite the hopeful efforts of the local tourism authority, which seems these days to be intent on turning the local leprosarium into a tourist village. As leprosariums go it is quite nice, situated gorgeously by the ocean and replete with coffee shops and restaurants run by the lepers themselves. But as a tourist attraction I think it's a bit of a tough sell.

In his younger days, Thay Chau had constructed a tower dedicated to Amitabha Buddha, the Buddha of the Western Paradise. It is an idiosyncratic pagoda, just across the road from the supermarket. When I visited his temple it happened to be the special festival day for Amitabha Buddha, so the tower was the focus of attention. Young monks were clambering all over it, scaling its eaves to brush them free of cobwebs and affix quantities of fairy lights ready for the evening's celebration. I watched with some trepidation as they climbed up the precarious tower in their rubber flip-flops. There was a sudden shout as one of the monks stumbled and nearly pitched to his death, but he managed to clutch onto the snout of the large concrete dragon that was weaving its way up the tower and was safe.

Hearing that something grand was being planned for the Amitabha feast day, a laywoman had offered to pay for the main hall to be cleaned and renovated. Wisely, the abbott had engaged an outside team of tradesmen to do this job, as the undisciplined monks would have made a game of it all and probably botched things terribly. The hall, a beautifully spacious 300-year-old building, was emptied of years of junk, while half a dozen men worked on polishing the tiles, cleaning the shrines and repainting the walls in the distinctive old-fashioned blue that covers so many Vietnamese interiors.

I was shocked to see that the main shrines, with their enormous statues, were covered with young workmen touching up areas where the paint had chipped and faded. They had had the respect to remove their shoes, but it was still something of a wrench to see the sacred figures so blithely manhandled.

The younger novices and the various orphans and layabouts that populate any provincial Buddhist temple were set to work on the little jobs that tend to be neglected during the rest of the year. Some were scouring out the dozens of mismatched vases that held the floral offerings of worshippers, many of which were in a ghastly state. Another was dusting then repainting the little wooden folding stands used to hold the *sutras,* the books of holy scriptures from which the community chanted.

I was rather at a loss as to what to do to help. I am inclined to be clumsy at the best of times, and if I offered to do anything practical Vietnamese people tended to fall into a frenzy of effort in order to stop me, presumably because I am a guest. As the monks ran about spring cleaning, chubby Abbott Chau detected my unease and kindly collected me for a walk. Now, it's not every day that a short and very fat Buddhist monk is seen walking down the streets of Quy Nhon hand in hand with a tall, very fat Western man. Both of us with shining bald pates and smiling, chubby cheeks, Abbott Chau's head finished just below where my chest began. People cheered, people jeered, and a small crowd of children collected around us, wanting to be in on the travelling show. 'But you could be brothers!' cried out old ladies from their shops as the abbott and I strolled past. 'Ah, but he is so much more handsome,' Abbott Chau would respond gallantly.

As the people of Binh Dinh province are known for their religious fervour, the short road hosted a number of other temples and churches. At the end of the street was a large and imposing temple, built in an exquisitely—if not alarmingly—eclectic jumble of Japanese and Tibetan Buddhist architecture, and that of the nearby Hindu towers of the ancient Champa kingdom that had once ruled this area. Thay Chau told me that the revered octogenarian abbott here was a noted herbalist. As we spoke, a young man was brought in suffering terrible pain from a broken leg. He had just been in a motorcycle accident and his friend carried him into the temple, screaming for the Abbott. Two nurse monks came out and spirited them away.

In a squat tower roofed in green tiles, the old abbott himself was seated at the head of a small parliament of middle-aged monks, all wizened and sun-blackened, and all of them smoking. They stood up as we entered and the abbott, a truly beautiful old man, insisted I sit right next to him in what was clearly a position of honour.

He began to quiz me about my religious orientation and daily habits. In his presence I felt the awe and excitement of being with someone who was indisputably wise and perfectly humble. There was not an ounce of pretension about him. He was clothed in the same scruffy old yellow shirt and brown pyjama pants that any low-ranking monk might wear to do the gardening. He was blissfully happy and utterly at ease.

As he took my hand in his, I felt the soft warmth of his wrinkled palms and fingers. They were the hands of a healer and of someone so completely gentle that no creature could ever fear him.

'All you need to remember, child, is to recite the Buddha's name.' He beamed at me with his toothless mouth and took a noisy sip of tea. 'That is all you ever need to worry about. Life is so difficult for foreigners. But if you chant the Buddha's name, his protection will always surround you.' At this he pulled from the pocket of his shirt a simple black plastic rosary and pressed it into my hands.

I took it from him and raised my palms to my forehead, thanking him using the simple monastic expedient of reciting the Buddha's name. He beamed at me again and turned back to the bench of old rogues, who were shuffling and snorting impatiently in their chocolate brown robes. I was dismissed.

ICE CREAM IN
QUY NHON

My friend Thay Quang had arrived, ostensibly to collect me and take me to his legendary little monastery by the sea.

Vietnamese is a complex language, and the observation of hierarchy and social relationships is essential in day-to-day speech. The simple terms of address 'you' and 'me' are, for example, almost never used. Instead one must work out one's relationship to the person being addressed and use the correct terms. Monks, for the most part, are addressed as *Thay*, which means teacher. Given names are rarely used, so it can make for an awkward situation when one walks into a monastery and calls out 'Thay!'

Thay Quang had taken up residence in a remote fishing village, and was constantly waxing lyrical about the charms of his little hamlet. But as often happens in Buddhist circles, things weren't quite working out as planned. My luggage had, that morning, been locked in a senior monk's quarters for safekeeping. That same monk had left for a distant temple in the faraway hills. I was trying not to panic on learning that he was completely uncontactable and not due to return for four days. My monkish friends were by contrast extremely relaxed. In that room was all my earthly goods, including essential medicines and toiletries, as well as all my clothes.

Unconcerned monks sat about in Abbott Chau's office drinking bottles of a sweet green-tea soft drink that had just hit the Vietnamese market. The monks assured me that the drink was extremely good for one's health, though after opening one of the warm bottles (the monks like to avoid ice, believing that it causes influenza) and taking a mouthful, I detected straight away that it probably contained as much sugar as a bottle of Coke. In a country with a rigidly controlled media, it is amazing how much advertising influences the Vietnamese. They don't seem yet to have any of the cynicism of Western consumers. Claims made about products, especially on television, are accepted holus-bolus.

'If the worse comes to worst, we can always bust open the elder monk's door,' suggested Thay Quang. This idea worried me. I had met the monk in question when we had left my things in his care. He was quite austere, to say the least. I could only imagine his reaction upon returning home to discover his room busted into.

At this point a very short young novice shuffled past the abbott's office. He was wearing brown pyjamas, the everyday uniform of monks all over Vietnam, but across his shoulders he'd thrown a saffron robe of the type and colour usually associated with the Theravadin monks more common in Cambodia and Thailand. He was wearing it in the manner of a shawl or scarf, and seemed quite confident in this sartorially peculiar combination. Thay Quang, the new arrival, nearly choked on his sweet green tea, and called out for the young monk to come back to the office this second. Abbott Chau merely beamed happily at his young charge.

'What on earth do you have on, monk?' Thay Quang demanded. 'You look like a Theravadin! You're not meant to have that on! Take it off right now.' In matters of dress monks are sticklers for tradition, and adopting the garb of a rival sect is simply beyond the pale.

The young monk, not at all concerned, tossed one of the ends of the robe across his throat and marched off, completely disregarding his senior. Thay Quang's eyes bugged out, and he turned to the abbott. 'What in God's name is he wearing that for?'

Thay Chau chuckled and said, 'Oh, he's back from a holiday in Thailand and it's just a little thing he's picked up.'

'But a monk just can't wear whatever he likes! What will people say?'

'Oh, they like it—they say it looks handsome.'

'Handsome!' snorted Thay Quang. 'What a disobedient child he is. You really should try to control these young monks more.'

'Oh, no harm done. He's quite charming, really. It doesn't matter if he wants to dress his habit up a little.' Thay Chau beamed proudly as he lit up a cigarette. 'All this renovation! Dust everywhere! It wreaks havoc on my asthma.'

While concerns about what was and was not appropriate for monks was debated, my luggage remained locked away. One of the young monks had been sent to gather whatever keys he could find on hooks and behind various doors throughout the temple complex. Some of those keys were ancient, huge and rusted, like pantomime props. None of them looked like they might fit the large, modern lock the senior monk had installed on his cell door. A couple of novices then set to work trying the various keys found in the lock. When none of them fitted they were sent back to try again. I wandered past them half an hour later. They smiled up at me, completely without malice at all the fuss and bother I was causing.

One of the monks, Nhuan, who seemed to be the abbott's right-hand man, was in charge of taking care of me. He drove into the cloister on a nice new motorcycle, holding out a helmet for me to wear. 'Come,' he said. 'We're going to the supermarket!'

The large supermarkets that take pride of place in Vietnamese towns of any size are not seen by the locals just as places to purchase day-to-day necessities. Indeed, most Vietnamese seem convinced that this is the place *not* to buy such things and willingly use the filthy traditional markets where they are invariably cheated by the stallholders. Supermarkets are entertainment venues, places to go and relax and take in the immense displays of attractive consumer goods. The phrase most commonly used is 'I'm going to the supermarket to play'. If you are hoping to buy that special gift for someone the supermarket is the place to head, and when the time arrives for giving the gaudily wrapped present is normally announced as having 'come from the supermarket'.

Nhuan's excitement was palpable as we pulled into the vast, hot parking lot of the Co-Op Mart on Le Duan street. The young attendants shrieked with joy at the sight of me seated behind the slight young monk. 'Heavens!' one shouted. 'Who's that skinny fellow behind you?' This was the kind of wit that I heard frequently back on the streets of Saigon. It seemed standard to state the exact opposite of something seen or experienced, and it never failed to be a crowd pleaser. If I was being driven past a restaurant, some young tough would shout out, 'Fuck my mother! Check out skinny Minnie on the back of that bike!' Once I came out of a temple to find a group of respectable and well-dressed young women holding one of my enormous shoes aloft and saying, 'Teensie-weensie, ain't it?'

So, true to form, Nhuan cracked up at this sharp repartee and slapped me hard on the back. 'Hear that, Brother? He said you were skinny!' And he guffawed all the way into the supermarket. Once at the threshold of the supermarket he became deadly serious, however, in case any undue levity might see us denied entry to the holy-of-holies—the low-rent, under-air-conditioned store selling a dizzying array of shabby Chinese electronic goods. Nhuan turned to me solemnly and, switching to English, he intoned, 'No smoking!' His eyes widened at the unbelievable sophistication of the concept. The formality of the surroundings obviously left Nhuan desperate for a smoke, however, for as soon as we had stepped out of the formal part of the supermarket and into the arcade of market-style stalls, he fired up a cigarette with obvious relief.

The back of the supermarket was an entertainment complex which looked out over a park running down to the beach. It was a beautiful aspect, and the hangar-like complex was filled with seafood restaurants as well as bars and coffee shops. All in all probably not the kind of place a monk should hang out in, but Nhuan clearly saw my presence as a kind of licence and he happily steered me into the seats outside an ice cream parlour. Without asking, the proprietor brought out two plates of the most delicious watery coconut ice cream, served in tiny scoops. Nhuan took a mouthful and gave a great theatrical shiver. 'Whooa! Now that's cold!' he said. I suggested that ice cream was meant to be a little on the cold side, but Nhuan dismissed my idea.

'I wouldn't normally eat something that cold, but since it's a special occasion . . .' He gingerly took another tiny spoonful and, placing it on his tongue, he swallowed it down and shook his head violently from side to side. 'Cold! Very, very cold!'

I had never witnessed such a reaction to ice cream before, and asked him what he expected it to taste like.

'Well . . . not this cold!'

The ice-cream parlour owner came out and greeted us in the traditional way, bowing and holding his palms at his chest. 'How is the ice cream, Thay?' he asked.

'Cold!' he responded, pushing his mostly uneaten portion away from him. The shopkeeper insisted on giving us our dessert free, reminding me again of the devoutness of the people of Quy Nhon. That's one of the nice things about being in a smaller provincial city: no shopkeeper in their right mind would give a monk a freebie in Ho Chi Minh City.

Going back to the parking lot, Nhuan refused to walk through the supermarket. 'Are you nuts?' he said. 'After what we just ate? You've gotta be kidding! Walking through that air-conditioning would kill us.'

Considering the air-con was running at what must have been thirty degrees I thought we could probably risk it, but Thay insisted we skirt the outside of the complex, stumbling over the unlandscaped paths that surrounded the concrete immensity of the building. The only other people in this no-man's-land were young ruffians, squatting on their haunches and smoking, intent on their mysterious business which seemed to consist largely of waiting. 'Hey, shorty!' they called out to me. 'What are you doing with the vegetarian? Is he your date?' Nhuan thought this was hilarious and chuckled all the way back to the motorcycle.

When we got back to the monastery, a waiting party was gathered outside the main hall for us. The abbott and Thay Quang were beaming, my luggage piled up in front of them. I was overjoyed. 'Did the old monk come back?' I asked. 'Or did you find the key?'

'Even better,' crowed the abbott, holding forth an enormous pair of bolt cutters. 'We just cut the lock in two! It only took a second.'

'Where have you been?' asked Thay Quang, impatient now to be going.

Nhuan pulled his helmet off and proudly told the gathered faithful that we'd just been to the supermarket. 'To have ice cream!' he added triumphantly.

'Ice cream!' shrieked Abbott Chau, clapping his hands at the very thought of it. 'How was it?' he demanded.

'Cold,' said Thay Nhuan, 'very cold.'

FISH, BEER
AND BANANAS

Thay Quang, my oldest friend in Vietnam, had grown plump. His had been a remarkable monastic career, marked by travel and education, and he possessed a doctorate from an Indian university. I still have never asked him the topic as I know I wouldn't understand it anyway. Despite his accomplishments—or perhaps because of them—Thay had decided to bypass the career path mapped out for him as an up-and-coming young monk and instead settle in a remote temple in the Binh Dinh countryside, taking possession of an old hillside shrine that had long been abandoned. Thay had told me that the setting was exquisite, high on a hill looking out over the ocean. The position was so remote that until recently the only way to get to the village had been by boat. In the past year the Vietnamese government had remedied this by building a road all the way out to the village from the city. This was all part of the development of this section of the province as a 'special economic zone'.

These zones were springing up all over Vietnam. It was difficult to imagine what might be constructed in these mysterious zones. Warehouses, one supposes, or factories. Thay Quang seemed to think that billiard halls might figure prominently in their make-up, and indeed the only functioning building in this man-made desert was a hangar-like snooker hall with one or two sad motorcycles standing outside it. But optimistic planning meant that many had stalled in their development, leaving vast areas of cleared wasteland inhabited by building teams with nothing to do but live in tents awaiting more money and the nod to go ahead with building. The Binh Dinh zone had suffered just such a fate. Once we crossed the new bridge out of Quy Nhon, buffeted by strong winds that threatened to throw us and my assortment of luggage off Thay's trusty old Honda, we entered a desert-like landscape with spookily deserted behemoths of land-moving equipment. It looked like something out of *Mad Max*. Dotted about were shacks made of pieces of iron and old rice bags. Sunburnt faces peered out from them at the sound of approaching traffic. A typhoon had also been through the region, and Thay warned me that the roads were a little ruined.

We were cruising through this devastation and Thay Quang called out, 'Welcome to Sahara!' Just as he did, there was a terrible explosion and the motorbike went into a spin, throwing me and my luggage into the sand.

'Oh dear!' called Thay. 'Are you all right? We must have driven over something. The tyre is totally blown out, I'm afraid.'

'How much further do we have to go?'

'Another fifteen kilometres?'

'What will we do?' I cried, more than slightly panicked. Never had I been so absolutely in the middle of nowhere, experiencing the kind of complete abandonment and isolation you would imagine would be impossible in a crowded country like Vietnam. Thay seemed unconcerned.

'No problem! I will push the bike back to Quy Nhon and have the wheel repaired. You just wait here.' I knew for a fact that the very rural outskirts of Quy Nhon were at least five kilometres back. As I looked around I saw nothing but the haze of thirty-five degree heat over the sea of sand and mud. 'Look!' said Thay happily. 'Over there—you can wait over there, it will be cool.' In the distance I could just about make out the outline of a massive truck or bulldozer. We gathered my things and trudged over. Once we got there I saw the barest sliver of shade on one side of the truck. I slunk into this and Thay waved goodbye. 'See you in an hour or two!' he said as I watched his grey-robed form disappear over the horizon, collecting his motorcycle on the way.

I had nothing to drink, and it was hot. My head pounded, and I wondered how long it would take to die of heat exhaustion in the circumstances. Then I heard someone calling.

'Hey! Big Brother! Over here! Come over here and rest!'

From what I had taken to be a pile of rubbish half-buried in the sand, a flap of a door had been opened. A man was waving at me. I hesitated. While I was almost certain they were honest workmen living in a makeshift camp, they could also have been squatters taking advantage of this unpoliced wasteland.

My mind leapt to the worst. I imagined them picking through my things while my corpse drained blood in the sand behind their shack.

'Oh, no!' I said, in my most polite Vietnamese. 'I'll be just fine here.'

'You'll die out there in this heat. Come over here and sit and rest.'

'Oh, no. I'll be just fine. Really, it's quite cool out here.'

The man sighed and came outside into the sun, walking toward me. He seemed enormous, shabbily dressed and very dark. Without a word he leaned forward and picked up my things and walked back toward the shack. I had no choice but to follow. He threw my things inside onto the floor and I entered behind him. It was a darkened room, filled with hammocks and a half-dozen shirtless, sweating men of various ages. It was very, very hot. One of the men remonstrated with my saviour and told him to take my luggage off the floor. A space was cleared on their only table, and all of my things were piled up on it.

'Have some water,' said one of the men, handing me a plastic mug.

'Would you like some fruit?' asked another, handing me a whole bunch of tiny green bananas. They all sat or lay swinging in their hammocks, staring at me, no-one saying a word. I could only imagine how extraordinary my appearance must have seemed to them. I explained why I was there and what had happened. They seemed uninterested. An extremely taciturn young man squatted in front of a sizzling wok, a cigarette in one corner of his mouth, stir-frying fish over a wood fire with an enormous pair of chopsticks. Like all the others he was shirtless, but his body was entirely covered from his neck to his waist with the most exquisite tattoos. Though all the men were darkened by working constantly in the sun this one was several shades blacker still, and I guessed he might be Cham or a member of one of the other ethnic minorities. The others noticed me staring, and one of them said, 'That's Van. He's our wife,' and they all laughed. Van didn't make a sound, just stared angrily into the hot, smoking oil and cooked his fish.

Soon lunch was served, inevitably with beer. I was cordially invited to join them. As lunch was nothing more than the fried fish with coarse, cheap rice and more of the bananas I'd been given, I refused. They pressed me, but the older man who had come to save me held up a hand and they were silenced. 'Didn't you see who he came here with? The monk from over the hill. Respect the man's religion—of course he can't eat fish! Here,' he said, plonking down in front of me a fresh hand of the tiny green fruit. 'Have some bananas.'

When we eventually made it to Thay's temple it was twilight. And though it may well have been exquisitely placed, we were both too exhausted to appreciate the views. It was almost time for evening prayers, and Thay had no time even for dinner. I was hastily shown a room in the guest quarters, which were positioned on a terrace overlooking the ocean. Worshippers had already begun arriving for the service, and the village elders had fired up a CD of Buddha recitation. The new arrivals took their places quietly on the temple floor and fell into the rhythm of the chanting almost immediately. The sound of their quavering, elderly devotions wafted up onto my terrace. Exhausted, stressed and hungry though I was, I knew it was my duty to freshen up and head back down to the prayer hall for an hour's chanting.

Though I'd made an effort to wash my face and scrub the worst of the mud and filth off my clothes, I still represented a sorry sight as I walked down the stairs to the Buddha hall. There were twenty or so devotees chanting when I got there. But, within minutes, there were thirty, and then forty. By the time the drum was struck for the entrance of the abbott, there were more than a hundred people in attendance. I suppose there's nothing else to do in a sleepy fishing village on a weeknight.

Thay Quang, of course, was otherwise engaged, being the abbott and the only resident monk. The disciples all tried to push me to the front of the hall, to the position of importance right behind the row of elders. But my head and body ached, my throat was dry, and I was so desperately hungry I felt like crying. Quite rudely I insisted on remaining in my place outside on the temple veranda. Entering the hall dressed in his golden ceremonial robes, Thay Quang looked a million dollars, as though he'd spent the day relaxing and maybe watching some TV. He shot me a sneaky, dazzling look and an even more dazzling smile that, though out of place in the ritual surroundings, was an immense act of compassion all of its own.

When everyone settled onto the floor to begin the recitation of that night's chapter of the *Lotus Sutra*, I closed my eyes and let the sound wash over me. This Sutra is seen as being the pinnacle of Buddhist revelation, the one Sutra that unifies all schools and sects, and Buddhist congregations normally chant their way through it a couple of times a year.

Reading the Sutra in translation, it is difficult to fathom its appeal. As is common in ancient texts based on oral traditions it is exceedingly repetitive, and large chunks of it are taken up with listing the various gods, goddesses, bodhisattvas, angels and mythical creatures who are present when the teachings are being given. Further pages are taken up with extolling the qualities of these same beings, and describing the clothes they are wearing or the jewelled lands they inhabit. In fact, actually gleaning some message or substance from the text requires an almost superhuman feat of excavation among the descriptive dross that otherwise bogs it down.

The ocean breeze blew up over the veranda, and I took out my rosary and began running the cool beads through my fingers. The moment in the liturgy came for Thay to stand and intone in a sing-song voice all the names of people and situations specially singled out to be blessed. It was a list of the usual suspects—the Vietnamese nation, the elders and people of the village, the various names of locals who had recently passed away. The archaic Vietnamese being sung in a ceremonial accent was almost incomprehensible to me, but right at the end, before the collected faithful fell to the floor in an act of communal obeisance and blessing, Thay called for the blessing of me, his foreign visitor.

And only then did I begin to cry.

THE CAN THO
FEAST OF ASKING

I was molested on the Thanh Nhan speedboat to Can Tho. It wasn't a traumatic experience. The late middle-aged chap responsible was really quite sweet and affable. But nonetheless I found it unnerving to have my genitals manhandled in broad daylight on the back of a speedboat, in full view of the chain-smoking French matrons who were my fellow travellers. The Thanh Nhan is meant to be an express boat, picking up passengers at the pier across from the Majestic Hotel in downtown Saigon and dropping them off three hours later in Can Tho, right in the heart of the Mekong Delta. But like all such promises in Vietnam, this one is subject to slight changes in detail, if not in intent, and even the best-laid plans are open to the manipulations of corruption. And so our express speedboat made several stops along the way, including one to pick up two respectably dressed gents at some unnamed village along the river. They risked life and limb clambering into the boat from the crowded concrete pier, the villagers joining in with the boat attendants in an effort to keep the vessel from smashing into the concrete sidings and sending us all to a watery grave.

The men were dressed in ties and carried briefcases—always an unsettling sight and normally, in Vietnam at least, an augury of bad things to come. The older of the two, with salt-and-pepper hair and a substantial moustache, sent his junior to sit in the enclosed cabin with everyone else. Peculiarly, he adopted to sit right next to me on the windy and frequently watery back deck, in the company of the French madames intent on their lung cancer. Fixing me with a smile, he placed a palm on my thigh and rubbed it heartily. This, I felt, was well within the acceptable realms of male-to-male contact in Vietnam. I was, after all, a rather large foreigner, and the friendly Vietnamese are frequently affectionate to a fault when confronted with someone who excites their curiosity. The hand stayed there for the next twenty minutes or so, and occasionally we would smile at each other.

It really is a remarkable trip, one which I heartily recommend to any traveller. The back deck is cool and comfortable, and the river is alive with activity: children swimming, people fishing. One can take in the temples and churches and municipal buildings, constructed to take advantage of the river views and the easy access that river travel provides. Barge boats act, rather terrifyingly, as mobile petrol stations, and their proprietors sit proudly smoking next to the vast tanks of fuel. Occasionally the boat's turbines get choked with river weed, and the vessel comes to a sudden—indeed, violent—halt. It was at one of these stops that my new gentleman friend slid his hand up to my crotch and grabbed at whatever he found there.

A boat is certainly the best, most comfortable and most picturesque way to get from Ho Chi Minh City down to the Mekong Delta. In the Vietnamese way the price of the ticket can be mercurial, and arriving on any given day the cost of the fare may have been hastily adjusted, scrawled in by hand on an otherwise official ticket. There is no point querying it. The ticket seller will merely feign ignorance and simply repeat, 'New price.' It is easy as a tourist to get heated up about such things in Vietnam; after a while one begins to feel exploited. But I really do advise people not to take it personally. Cheating has nothing to do with race or perceived gullibility, and everything to do with traditional Vietnamese attitudes to class, wealth and social status. Even local Vietnamese, if they present themselves as privileged in any way, are subject to impromptu taxes on their wealth. In traditional village life in Vietnam, the wealthy were always obliged to share their fortune whenever they were asked, and such an attitude was only ever strengthened by the nominally Marxist ideas of the new Vietnam.

To some people my molestation might seem a cut-and-dried case of moral outrage, but I was brought up a well-mannered country boy, which meant never to make a scene. I also happened to know that among Vietnamese men the groping of genitals was a not uncommon form of jocularity. Once in Hanoi I approached a taxi rank and was confronted by a driver who reached down and gave my genitals a thorough going-over, reporting on their dimensions to his fellow drivers. This was universally seen as an hilarious piece of good fun, and my willingness to also see it as such made me instantly one of them. For the rest of my stay I was feted by Hanoi taxi drivers as the good-time guy who allowed his penis to be fondled by old Mr Thoi. So I wasn't yet ready to condemn my travelling companion as an out and out pervert. I just smiled sweetly and removed myself from his grasp, thinking I would simply be the funny story he could tell his buddies at the veterans' club that night. I was imagining the guffaws that would greet him on reaching the part where he said, '. . . and then I grabbed his balls!'

But if I was going to be that night's joke, it was turning out to be a long-winded one. Pretty soon I again felt that familiar hand on my thigh, this time high enough up to make even me uncomfortable. And this time the boat barely rocked as it passed another ferry, but still my friend lurched exaggeratedly and went for the full handful once more. 'Old Uncle,' I demurred politely. 'Please, I am a little embarrassed.' I gestured at the French ladies, who were watching us in utter fascination.

'You speak Vietnamese!' he said, his eyes sparkling, but his hand kept solidly in place. 'What a clever boy. Bet you've got a big one, too. Tell me, is your body covered in hair?'

Oddly enough, such prurient curiosity about foreign bodies is also not uncommon in Vietnam. For all their famed modesty, the Vietnamese can be disarmingly frank about body parts and sexual function. The old lady who cleaned the kindergarten across the road from my house in Ho Chi Minh City greeted me almost every day with an obscene reference to my dick. One morning she grabbed a metre-long plastic crayon, of the kind used to do promotions in stationery stores, and held it to her groin in imitation of my mythic endowment. This amused the straitlaced young kindergarten teachers no end. So this time I simply pushed his hand away and smiled in feigned ignorance—my usual reaction to such ribaldry.

'So you're off to Can Tho, then,' he said. The Vietnamese propensity to state the obvious in the name of social interaction is always dumbfounding. People will often pull up a chair at my table while I have a mouthful of noodles and say, 'I see you're eating, huh?' In cafés waiters will pull a book out of my hands and ask, 'Reading a book, Big Brother?'

'I betcha you've got a wife or two in Can Tho. I know what foreigners are like!'

'Um, actually, I'm going to attend a friend's engagement party.'

'Oh ho ho, is that what they're calling it these days? Can't fool me, Little One, there's only one reason someone like you would be going to Can Tho.'

'No, really, I am visiting a friend.'

'Yes indeed, lots of lovely little friends,' he winked lasciviously at me. 'Of course, in Can Tho one can easily make friends with girls *and* boys . . .'

'My friend is a man.'

'Ha! Just as I thought. I know you foreigners run easily on petrol *and* diesel.'

I laughed at this wonderfully industrial metaphor and, taking advantage of my mirth, the old businessman went in for another grope.

DON'T PAY THE FERRYMAN'S WIFE

Ricky is a friend from Saigon. Standing almost six feet tall, Ricky is an enthusiast of body building and is a young executive—one of the new breed of Vietnamese yuppies who will be the future of the nation. Ho Chi Minh City is his plaything, and he is part of that city's elite. Paid a high salary and eligible for four weeks vacation a year, Ricky inhabits a rarefied world that revolves around the latest nightclubs, imported designer clothing and package tours to Thailand. We only ever converse in English, and when we go to restaurants together he insists on ordering in English—with often disastrous consequences. With his size and attitude, people frequently mistake Ricky for a 'Viet Kieu', an overseas Vietnamese. This kind of mistake delights him.

Ricky had been mentioning for some weeks that his sister, another upwardly mobile young Saigonese, was to celebrate her engagement party at their family's orchard in a village outside of Can Tho. When I agreed to come I think he went into a panic, morphing into Dang, the third-from-last child of an enormous Mekong Delta family which had traditionally eked a living growing oranges and longans in the bucolic south. Too late I realised my arrival would also prove a logistical nightmare. The already crowded family home was not comfortable at the best of times, and the presence of a fussy foreigner was the last thing people wanted during a busy family celebration.

Engagement parties are part of the series of seriously expensive rites of passage that make up traditional Vietnamese social life. Usually defined by the name *Dam* (feasts or banquets), these long-winded parties mark the usual hatch, match and despatch occasions familiar to any family. Baby's birthday parties, weddings, funerals, memorials—these are all of necessity celebrated with much ado. The engagement banquet is normally considered a time for young people to mix and live it up a little with their peers, and the festivity, associated with much ritual, is called the *Dam Hoi*—the Feast of Asking. It is when the potential groom's family makes a ritual visit accompanied with symbolic gifts wrapped elaborately in red cellophane and served up on lacquered red boxes hired specially for the occasion. In the Delta engagement parties are serious, multi-day celebrations, with different guests arriving and leaving in shifts and food constantly being cooked, prepared and served.

Even getting to the village proved something of an endurance test. Ricky's young nephew, a business student from Ho Chi Minh City with a passion for multi-level marketing, was sent to collect me from the high-speed ferry in Can Tho city.

From there we walked down the esplanade to the main commuter quay.

The esplanade along the river in Can Tho is really quite beautiful, if humble. The only thing that mars it is the scores of touts and shysters impressing upon you the urgency of taking a boat tour/finding a hotel/going to meet some nice girls. Can Tho is really the sinful pearl in the Mekong Delta's crown, and the prevalence of so much prostitution is quite a surprise in such a seemingly sleepy place. We were pursued all the way down to the commuter quay by a half-crazed crone offering to show us a variety of services and leisure opportunities, from seafood restaurants to brothels.

Most serious transport in Can Tho and its surrounds is done by boat, as the waterlogged villages are the merest islands separated by bodies of water. In most cases, boats represent the only way to get around. The Amway-inspired nephew led me to one of the large commuter boats, a rickety bus-on-water with a sweaty collection of passengers jammed into an uncomfortable hull, all of them pulling the wooden shutters off the windows to let in some river breeze. As always in rural Vietnam, the boat filled up gradually with large quantities of freight—bags and bags of mysterious stuff, boxes of plasticware, live poultry tied together in bundles by their feet. It wasn't until half an hour or so had elapsed and the boat was uncomfortably crowded and thoroughly unseaworthy that we set off, despite the initial promise of the driver that we would be gone within five minutes.

Nothing could happen, of course, until the boat keeper's wife was on board. This extraordinary breed can be seen the length and breadth of Vietnam, and in truth it is probably a role as old as Vietnamese culture. In recent years the boat keeper's wife has morphed into the bus driver's wife, who serves a similarly vital role. This one was an almost textbook specimen. Extravagantly plump, she was dressed in the ubiquitous polyester pyjamas that all working-class women in Vietnam wear. Hers were in a vibrant print, and she wore suspended around her neck on a purple cord a money pouch. From this pouch she extracted a large bottle of imported Singaporean green liniment, and proceeded to apply it liberally to the back of her neck, her temples and upper lip. While doing this, I noticed the quantities of golden jewellery of the yellowest type clattering about her person. She was also quite made up—a rarity among working women in Vietnam, and a necessary marker of her exalted status.

The boat keeper's wife is really the executive manager, and her command is final. It is she who decides when the boat is full enough to set off, who negotiates the drop off of goods at various village piers and how much should be charged for such a service. Once we were sailing along the river she affected to chat to her husband briefly, and then shouted out some commands to her elderly mother looking after the children in the prow of the boat, which was replete with kitchen, laundry and pot plants. But everyone was on edge, waiting for her to begin the rounds of fare collection. It was an exhausting and time-consuming process, equal parts theatre and avarice. She began with the person immediately to her left. 'Well, Madame Nga, did you get time to eat lunch?'

'Not at city prices, Sister Hai! I'll have a late lunch at home.'

'Going home, then? Well, that will be 5000 dong.'

'Five thousand dong! Since when did they legalise robbery on the rivers? Coming here I only paid 2000.'

'Coming here you didn't have eight boxes of fish sauce and a whole pig carcass. Five thousand now, madame, or I'll be having that pig for my own dinner.'

And so it went on. Each passenger was assessed according to perceived wealth and social status, the quantity of goods they'd brought with them and several other, more esoteric, criteria. Enormous arguments ensued, though invariably every person disembarked with a cheery wave and a call of 'See you soon, Sister!' Each person had a story of poverty and hardship, and a series of ingenious reasons as to why they should be charged less. Big Sister Hai, the boat keeper's wife, had heard them all, however, and brooked no opposition. Once she'd worked out how much your fare should be, you paid it or swam home. By the time she got to me her hair was a little dishevelled and her face slightly dirty from the smoke of the boat's engine and the constant application of green oil to alleviate her headache.

'A foreigner?' she declared to my junior executive chaperone, as though noticing me for the first time. He smiled meekly, trying to conceal the carton of baby formula he'd brought on board. Silently he handed over two 5000 dong notes, which she completely ignored.

'That'll be 20,000,' she said, bearing the traces of a smile. Amway boy began to disagree, but Sister Hai fixed him with a glare and added, 'Each.'

CRAZY DELTA DANCING

There is much to be seen along the various tributaries of the Mekong that weave through this gloriously sultry part of southern Vietnam. People live their lives along the river, houses jut perilously out into the water, and churches and temples seem to have made a special effort to establish themselves along the riverbanks. I saw a little Protestant chapel with its own jetty and thought of how wonderful it must be to be a Baptist in Can Tho, taking a leisurely boat ride to church of a Sunday morning.

After about forty minutes on the river we arrived at Ricky's home village. Somehow I managed to hoist my substantial form up onto the high cement jetty from the low boat, and Ricky himself was there to greet us. This was not the Ricky I knew; the cocky, Westernised white-collar worker with a passion for dance music and red wine was gone. He had slid straight back into his familial role, and was dressed in long shorts and a polyester football shirt. He was also shoeless, which was wise because we had to travel along about a kilometre of muddy paths before we reached the orchard. He seemed embarrassed about the mud and the half-starved dogs that ran out of every farmhouse, fangs bared and snarling. Uncharacteristically, he spoke only in Vietnamese, though the mini-yuppie nephew kept up a running commentary in surprisingly good English.

Once at the farmhouse I was introduced to the whole family and to anyone else there for the afternoon's festivities—there seemed to be hundreds. A crowd of men were sitting under a boiling-hot marquee made out of romantic pink polyester. This was the venue for celebrations. The men were sweating like crazy in the dense afternoon heat, all of them stripped to the waist and drinking little cups of homemade rice spirit, accompanied by side dishes of dried squid and large chunks of pomelo dipped in chilli and salt.

Ricky had five brothers, and all of them were enormous in a way that is rare in Vietnam. Tall and garrulous, they could only be described as fat, their vast bellies stretching out taut and naked, their smooth skins glowing with sweat and alcohol. I was variously slapped and pinched in the hands-on fashion of drunken Vietnamese men, and a small plastic stool was found for me. Celebrations had well and truly begun, and from hereon in I was to be an essential part of them.

The drinking was perpetual; each night, whichever men found themselves still present at festivities would simply collapse under a huge mosquito net in the front room, snoring and retching till morning. On the day I arrived it was three in the afternoon and about forty-five degrees in that pink tent, so the last thing I felt like was a round or three of bootleg liquor and some sun-dried seafood. But social obligations are to be taken seriously in Vietnam, and my position as new guest of honour carried with it a significant set of expectations. For the next few days, I would have to remain well and truly drunk.

Ricky left me alone with the men and went to work in the kitchen with the women. His special role was to make hundreds of little coconut-flavoured sponge cakes, cooked in strange greased pans held over an open fire. When Ricky took me into the heavily populated, smoky kitchen a whole new posse of female relatives had arrived to help, though there were plainly already too many jammed in there. They ignored me and instead turned their attention to Ricky. 'I swear, you get more handsome each time we see you!' one of them said, slapping Ricky's enormous and painstakingly cultivated bicep. 'When will we be celebrating your engagement?' another asked, and Ricky snuck me an arch look. 'Thirty-six and still not married! It'll be too late soon!'

At this Ricky coughed and hurriedly changed the subject. Even taking into account the Vietnamese custom of adding a year or two to one's real age (at birth one is calculated to be a year old, and then another year is added at the first occurrence of the lunar New Year), this offhand statement let slip that Ricky was at least four years older than what he'd told me. I smiled at his vanity, but also felt a little sorry for him. Saigon was a big place filled with beautiful young people, and if a man was going to compete on the romantic marketplace he might need to adjust the truth a little here and there.

There were roving flocks of chickens and ducks that moved about the farm with a great degree of volubility, but knew when to keep a low profile. As celebrations progressed and more banquets were served, the flock began to shrink visibly. Ricky occasionally would swing by to gauge my progress and, frustratingly, instead of rescuing me he would pop open another bottle of rice vodka or hand over another small, roasted crustacean. 'You're here to have fun,' he would insist. 'You can just relax.'

But the event was anything but relaxing. I am an unusually private person, and in my day-to-day life I enjoy sustained periods of solitude where I can read and write and regain my energy. While at the engagement party this was absolutely impossible. I was public property and every single waking moment was spent in the company of others, drinking or listening to someone else's drunken rambling. At night I was expected to doss down in that crowded front room, slowly dying of heat exhaustion underneath the dense mosquito net, surrounded by comatose and variously farting male forms.

People began to call for me in the mornings. Hungover farm boys remembered their drunken pledges of undying friendship the night before, and came to wake me up at five in the morning and take me to have noodles or coffee at the village's only restaurant, causing me to pick my way over the snoring, fat bodies of Ricky's multitudinous brothers. At night the party would really pick up and an elaborate banquet would be served, along with large Coke bottles filled with a different kind of homemade alcoholic beverage, this one cloudy and lethal and almost guaranteed to cause nausea. We would be served bowls of tasty duck congee filled with big blocks of congealed duck's blood. I began to realise why those roving gangs of ducks and chickens seemed a little edgy. Platters of suckling pork were placed on the table, each piece almost entirely fat with just the thinnest layer of meat at the bottom.

After the banquet, Ricky would come forth as master of ceremonies and host a karaoke session. This entertainment was mostly dominated by the young women in the group, though occasionally a shy farm boy would venture forth, accompanied by shouts of derision from his drunken peers. Invariably the song would feature some embarrassingly overblown romantic allusion or, even worse, be sung from the point of view of a woman. At this the boys would hoot, and shout things like, 'Check out Quy! Up there singin' like a girl!'

Once the karaoke came to a natural close, the women would vanish and Ricky would begin playing a selection of dance songs. 'Come on now!' he'd call. 'It's time to dance.' At first one or two of Ricky's huge brothers would rush the dance floor, their enormous, sweaty torsos heaving roughly in time to the music. And then, extraordinarily, all of the village men would joyously wend their way up and start dancing. The younger men, by now elaborately drunk, would tear at their clothing and work themselves up into a frenzy of dancing, doubtless with the village girls watching invisibly from the darkened windows of the house.

In Vietnam, as in most parts of the world, dance music is owned by obscure producers of a furious kind of Euro-techno. The songs themselves have a certain intense sameness, and are rarely heard on the Top 40 charts in the West. Generally they are characterised by an easy-to-understand English lyric that changes from song to song, but could equally be interchangeable. So the village men gyrated variously to songs like 'I'm So Lucky, Lucky' and another memorable one, the lyrics of which went simply 'Hello, how are you?' over and over again in a mysteriously Austrian or Latvian accent. The village boys nearly exploded with joy when a song came on that chanted, over a heavy bass line, 'Sexy, sexy, sexy'. It was at this point that I was dragged up on the dance floor, where I was forced to boogie for an hour or more while elderly farmers brought me little glasses full of rice liquor which I had to skol in time to the music.

Ricky's city nephew, the one who was passionate about Amway, videoed the whole incident, and for all I know the evidence is still out there now on some obscure Vietnamese equivalent of YouTube. He edited it and uploaded it on the spot from his ridiculously high-tech telephone, and I believed he titled it, in English, *Crazy Dancing in Can Tho*.

DAD'S PLACE
ON THE MEKONG

In the heat of the next afternoon, Ricky wanted me to meet his father. 'I thought you said your father was dead?' I asked, perhaps a little insensitively.

'Oh, he is,' said Ricky. 'But this farm is still his.'

I never really learned the name of Ricky's village, some ten kilometres along the river outside of Can Tho. This often happens in Vietnam. Though people feel tied to their village roots—and even people who have lived in Saigon for generations will, when asked where they come from, give the name of some obscure southern village they barely know—when you visit these villages it is difficult to identify them. The communities are small, and the boundaries between the villages can sometimes be fluid. And no-one seemed to bother me, the foreign tourist, with the exact names of places. 'Oh, it's near Can Tho,' they would say.

On a little hill behind Ricky's farmhouse stood an enormous pagoda-like structure. I had noticed its elaborate roof poking up above the trees, and I thought it might be a neighbouring temple. But it turned out to be Ricky's father's mausoleum. Easily the size of a small house, the memorial structure was ornately and expensively built. It was fully tiled, and the grave at the centre was raised and featured a large portrait of the deceased. There was also a platform for burning incense and offering flowers and fruit. The whole structure was fenced in a rather fancy ornate stainless steel that was all the rage in southern Vietnamese buildings. Though open-sided, the whole mausoleum was immaculately clean and well kept, even though his father had been dead for five years or more.

Ricky opened the little gate and we went in. Putting his palms together at his chest, he bowed to the grave and said a silent little prayer, and I did the same out of respect. 'This is where he used to come,' explained Ricky, 'he and his friends. They would come out here and drink rice whisky, and when they got too drunk my mother would send us out with a big mosquito net which we would rig up between the trees. I have happy memories of this place.'

Ricky lay down on the cool tiled floor, careful to direct his feet away from his father's headstone. He tapped the floor beside him, and I lay down too. 'I can't imagine what your life would be like,' he said. 'I am lucky. I have money, and I have travelled. But only to places like Thailand and Malaysia. Sure, things are better there than in Vietnam, but if I wander even just a few streets from my hotel I can see people living in exactly the way people live here. I know at heart that they have shared the same experiences. I can understand them. But you, what must it be like in your country? Free school, free medicine, no poverty, no crime. I can't imagine what it would be like to live without fear.'

'But we have fear, too. Life is difficult wherever you go.'

'Oh, you say that, but I think you don't really believe it. I must worry each and every day of my life. If something goes wrong in my life, I just die—there is nothing to protect me. But you, you don't need to worry. You have good karma.'

The hot afternoon air was thick around us. I was sweating through my cotton shirt onto the elaborate tiled floor of a family mausoleum. I would never build such a thing for my parents, and no-one would ever build one for me.

But in spite of that, I knew that Ricky was right. Life had been good for me. I had nothing to fear.

FEEDING THE CHICKENS

The usual Mekong Delta toilet is a difficult thing for a man of my size to negotiate. Most farms also feature small fish farms, deepish dams that contain any number of snapping fish and eels. These creatures are grown to amazing size using only the very best food that Mother Nature can provide. A long and waving bamboo jetty juts out into the middle of these dams, and at the very end is a small, semi-enclosed platform. From this platform you squat, and try to ignore the sound of fish slapping at the water beneath you. You also hope that fish won't be on the lunch menu—but it invariably is.

Ricky's orchard, being the country seat of a middle-class Saigon family, had somewhat revamped the traditional toilet. The jetty was made of concrete, and the platform, though still only tall enough to be able to hide the barest minimum of me, was made of brick. It was also very, very small. Soon after my arrival I enquired about the toilet, and Ricky waved noncommittally toward the back of the property. I took one look at it and knew I would never fit in that little brick enclosure.

I rushed back and drew my friend aside. 'Um, Ricky, we have a little problem here. I don't fit in the toilet.'

'Of course you will! You have seen my brothers. They all fit in fine.'

'Maybe, but there's Vietnamese big and then there's Western big. I'm still a lot bigger than those guys. And besides, they're used to . . . uh . . . squatting.' Ricky rolled his eyes. Just like a foreigner to be so precious when he had coconut cakes to make.

'Well,' he said, 'that's the only one there is. Either you go there or you find a nice quiet spot out under the pomelo trees.'

Ordinarily this would have been an option, but the farm was crawling with relatives and every time I ventured into the orchard I was invariably followed by a team of young children fascinated by my every move or, worse still, the roving flock of various poultry. As the need grew more and more dire I ventured further and further afield, but each time I stumbled upon a troupe of young girls eating limes, or Ricky's nephew decided to come for a walk and pick my brains about Anthony Robbins. 'So, do you think he'll ever come to Vietnam? I really wanna see that guy.'

Fortunately, I had my usual stash of anti-diarrhoea medication, and I just kept swallowing those. I figured it couldn't do me any harm. At the end of the first night I was feeling a little bloated and, what with all the drinking and feasting, my breath was starting to smell funny. On a reconnaissance mission through the house I discovered that there was another toilet situated in a boxy, makeshift room, somewhat unsanitarily in the very middle of the kitchen. 'No, you can't use that,' said Ricky. 'It's for my mother, and the other women. If you use it they'll just listen to you and talk about you.' I could see that he had a point. At any given time the kitchen had about a hundred women inside it, many of them with nothing to do but shoot the breeze. I could see that my use of the women's bathroom would cause a minor fuss, and would be talked about for days.

The second day one of the villagers took me to his house, and I thought I'd take the opportunity. 'So,' I asked casually. 'Have you got a toilet here?'

'Sure we do!' he said, escorting me proudly around the back. There was a single piece of bamboo leading out over a pond, ending in a platform sunk into the water. This baby didn't even have walls.

'Nice toilet!' I said cheerily. 'Just wanted to see it!'

I came back to Ricky's and swallowed down another handful of Imodium with rice whisky to stop any urges. I was starting to feel sick.

By the afternoon of the second day I was feeling desperate. I had low-grade alcohol poisoning and the accompanying dehydration, and 24-hour party food was not sitting well on my engorged stomach. I had noticed the men's shower block, a simple but private brick shed with a woven palm-leaf roof. When I went in for a shower I discovered that it was furnished with a couple of hooks, a big ceramic urn full of cool, fresh water with a plastic scoop floating in it, and a fist-sized hole where the floor met the wall. The water drained out of this hole almost straight into the dam, there being only a small drain of about thirty centimetres running through the mud from the shower enclosure directly into the fish farm. The fish were already eating shit. If I just endeavoured to thoroughly clean the shower enclosure after I was finished . . . I saw a solution to my problem.

Grabbing my towel and soap, I casually told Ricky, 'I'm just going to take a shower.'

'But you just showered a couple of hours ago.'

'I know, but it's kinda hot. I've been sweating all morning.'

'Sure,' he said, pulling a fresh batch of cakes out of the fire. 'Do whatever you want.'

I ran into the shower room, stripped and let nature take its course. I was incredibly relieved, and quite impressed with my own ingenuity and subtlety. This was all running perfectly. I took a scoop of water and set about flushing out the room. And then the terrible noise started. I don't know if you've ever heard a mixed flock of ducks and chickens engaged in a feeding frenzy, but it's noisy. Very noisy.

'What the hell?' I heard Ricky's mother come out into the yard. I could see through that drainage hole that dozens of birds were flocking to the short stretch of mud on the banks of the dam, intent on getting their own little piece of whatever they found so nice. 'What are those ducks doing back there? I've never seen them like this.'

I was madly throwing water through the hole, attempting

to swill away the evidence, but those birds were enjoying themselves too much. 'Are they eating the shower water?' asked Ricky's elderly mother, her voice genuinely puzzled. Some of the children must have come out to investigate more closely.

'Eeuw!' I heard one of them cry. 'The chickens are eating shit! Someone shit in the shower.' By now all the little baby chickens and ducks had joined in, and I heard their merry chirping in the shower recess.

'Ricky!' cried one of the myriad aunts, just outside the bathroom door. 'Come quickly. Your foreign friend's just shit in the shower!'

GRANDMOTHER'S SECRET

In Saigon I had never really asked Ricky about his religion. I guess I assumed that, like so many young professionals who had grown up as good Communists during a time when the system was at its most hard-line, he simply had no interest in the subject. One morning, things were a little quiet and the new round of celebrations was yet to begin. In fact, the long anticipated groom-to-be and his family were expected to arrive in a fleet of boats sometime before lunch. 'Would you like to visit my granny?' asked Ricky, and I jumped at the chance. I knew that if anyone discovered me wandering around the party house alone they would force more alcohol on me. The Vietnamese have no taboos about drinking before noon; if it's party time, it's party time.

Grandma lived about a kilometre away, along a series of narrow, muddy paths wending through various farms and orchards. People called out to us and greeted Ricky. Ricky's size and good looks were frequently commented on, and even people he didn't know would freeze in their tracks and say, '*Troi oi!* So handsome!' He explained that his grandmother—his deceased father's mother—lived in her own orchard, cared for by two spinster daughters. She was also very, very old. When we arrived I discovered she lived in a large and handsome wooden house, built in the traditional style. It would once have been the most beautiful house in the village, but by now its wooden panels were warped and cracking, the massive dark, wooden furniture deemed hopelessly out of style. It was the kind of furniture that would sell for $10,000 a piece in Australia as oriental antiques, but which the people of the Delta regularly chop up for firewood.

The house was unexpectedly full of people, all women well over 'a certain age'. His smiling aunts ushered us in and gave us cakes and cups of Milo. A great fuss was made over getting me a chair that wouldn't break under my weight, even though all the chairs in the room were quite substantial. A chair that must have weighed a good fifty kilos and resembled a throne was dragged out from some obscure back room, and everyone agreed that this was the only one in the house suitable for the job. Grandma sat in state on her large wooden bed. These beds are frequently the main piece of furniture in country households, and serve not only as places to sleep on but places to eat and entertain. Elderly people who have retired from active work can seem to spend their entire lives on them. True to form, Ricky climbed up on the bed to visit with his grandmother, pushing aside the various gifts that the other guests had brought, as well as the other guests themselves.

Grandma was dressed in glowing white pyjamas, as were the spinster aunts. Indeed, all of the guests (and I couldn't fathom why there were so many) were dressed in the same elegant all-white ensemble. I peeked into the glass-fronted wardrobe that stood by the matriarch's bed and saw row after row of white clothing. What a peculiar style, I thought to myself. Perhaps she is still in some elaborate phase of mourning, white being the colour of grief in Vietnam. Ricky followed my gaze and scooted off the bed and took me in hand. 'Come with me,' he said, opening one of the carved wooden wall panels. As we stepped through we entered a concealed room, and inside was the most elaborate home shrine I had ever seen. More than a shrine, the room was a fully decked-out hall of Cao Dai worship, furnished with the necessary shrines and images. It would comfortably have seated a dozen worshippers. Suddenly the white clothing and the improbable presence of so many people made sense. Ricky's grandma was the local Cao Dai priestess.

Cao Dai is an indigenous Vietnamese spiritualist sect that was once one of the most powerful political forces in southern Vietnam. Whole areas of the south converted to the religion in its heyday during the 1950s, and its peculiarity and colourful attempts at unifying different religions has intrigued Western writers and historians since its inception. The Caodaists attempted to universalise the religious experience through combining the doctrines of Buddhism, Confucianism, Taoism and Catholicism, and inventing their own peculiar mythology. For the follower, Cao Dai is simply the inevitable conclusion of centuries of religious exploration in the East and the West. It is not a matter of complexity or even argument, for as the Cao Dai *Canonical Codes* state, 'All human beings have to recognise what is over our heads.'

'I didn't know you were Cao Dai,' I said to Ricky.

'Oh, well, I don't really like to talk about it. People in Saigon don't understand. They think we are weird.' I, too, felt embarrassed, because the whole time I had been in Vietnam I had been researching Cao Dai in depth, and would regularly bore Ricky with mini-lectures about my discoveries.

'And your grandmother?'

'Yes, she knows all there is to know about Cao Dai. She has been the highest-ranking Caodaist around here for many years. In truth, there aren't that many of them left any more. Just our family and the women outside.'

'But what about you, and your brothers? Do you ever worship?'

Ricky looked guilty. 'No—it's so hard, and so boring. And so many days to be vegetarian! You know I go to the gym every day—I could never afford to eat vegetarian food so often. I would lose condition.'

On the way back I thought about Ricky and his new concerns, and how they overshadowed the old. He was very excited about my impending visit to Tay Ninh, the holy capital of the Cao Dai faith. I now understood why he kept telling everybody about it. He had never made the trip. 'It's too hot there, and I have heard the hotels are below par. But a lot of people have been talking about that new supermarket that has opened up there . . .'

Ricky's world was one of more concrete dreams and hopes, goals that bypassed the mystical temperament of his forefathers. He wanted his own house in one of the new estates opening up on the outskirts of Saigon. He wanted to travel, to look strong and beautiful; to have a foreign, rich or glamorous partner—hopefully all three. None of these goals sat easily with the otherworldly scope of his ancestral religion. He viewed his spiritual inheritance with more than a little embarrassment. He saw it as a kooky, provincial cult, something best left unmentioned. And yet he ached for the spiritual.

One day we were shopping in one of Saigon's enormous downtown book emporiums, and I discovered with joy that they stocked some of Louise L. Hay's books translated into Vietnamese. I bought these for Ricky, along with a Vietnamese-language copy of Eckhart Tolle's *The Power of Now* and Swami Yogananda's autobiography. Ricky was delighted, and soon Ms Hay's inspirational tome *I Can Do It!* became his little bible. He read sections of it daily, and used its affirmations while he was working out furiously at the gym.

In a way I felt sad. The Cao Dai religion had its own rich literature, indeed it was founded as an act of spiritualist automatic writing, and I was certain that within its prayers hid any number of uplifting phrases that Ricky could recite during his curls and squats. But I had unwittingly become a spiritual imperialist, facilitating the replacement of a distinctly Vietnamese religious tradition with the global patois of American self-help.

TAY NINH *OI*!

Apart from the obligatory day trip to see the Caodaists at prayer, nobody ever really seems to visit Tay Ninh. The hotels are cavernous and empty, occasionally host to a single, mysterious visitor from China, always dressed oddly at breakfast. Really, Cao Dai, the celebrated invented religion of Vietnam, *is* the city of Tay Ninh, and vice versa.

Caodaists call God the Jade Emperor, or the High Tower. God is an essence, not ever properly described. The town of Tay Ninh, about ninety minutes' drive from Ho Chi Minh City, is entirely devoted to this peculiar cult of Cao Dai, the wholly Vietnamese religion that elevates Charlie Chaplin to sainthood and was once one of the greatest independent military powers in Vietnam.

It is odd to arrive in a place where almost everyone you meet follows the same religion, and accepts it unquestioningly.

These days the followers of Cao Dai in Tay Ninh are a pretty laid-back bunch. The younger members were fiercely proud of their religion. They saw themselves as special, and at odds with the values of most of the rest of contemporary Vietnamese society. I befriended a young man called Linh, a somewhat louche hairdresser, fashion designer and—mostly—waiter. Linh's concerns seemed to be overwhelmingly this-worldly. But when I questioned him about his religion he grew quite emotional. 'I am not like the other Vietnamese you will meet,' he said. 'I am someone *co dao*, a man with strong religious beliefs.' The fact that he was throwing down an icy cold bottle of Heineken in a crowded Saigon nightclub at the time he made this statement seemed not to detract from it. I had encountered no other young Vietnamese quite so ready to admit to the strength of their spiritual beliefs.

Linh was tall and strongly built, his face lantern-jawed and bony. In the West he would be considered devastatingly handsome, but in Vietnam his features were seen as a little too harsh, his square face indicative of a lack of gentleness. He promised to take me to Tay Ninh, the Holy City, which was his home town. 'There is no other place like Tay Ninh,' he said, growing a little teary. 'It is the most sacred place in all of Vietnam.'

If you are not on a day-trip organised by one of the tour companies, getting to Tay Ninh is no easy feat. Linh was sceptical about the bus. 'But it will be fun!' I insisted, as we headed to the An Suong bus station.

The bus station turned out not to be for the faint of heart. Most passengers bypassed the official government ticket booth with its set fares and walked straight up to the privately owned buses waiting at the station, negotiating their own fare with the driver or with his plump wife, who was invariably seated right by the door. My faith in things official still intact, I approached the government ticket booth and bought the regulated ticket to Tay Ninh on the next departing bus. When I walked to the vehicle pointed out begrudgingly by the young woman behind the counter, the driver's wife, an enormously obese woman, sent me straight back to the ticket booth. 'A man of your size!' she screeched, though her own bottom easily doubled mine in girth. 'You have to buy two tickets.' Chastened, I returned with two tickets, and she happily directed me towards a single narrow seat.

'When does the bus leave?' I asked.

'Oh,' she said, waving her hand in the air and affecting a mysterious manner. 'In the next five minutes . . . or so.' The 'or so' was an ominous add-on that I had grown to know and hate in Vietnam.

It was about forty-five degrees in the little minibus standing in the sun in the insanely crowded bus station. I felt a hard whack on my shoulder and, turning to source it, saw an elderly woman standing outside the bus pushing a baguette through the window. 'Buy some bread, Little Brother,' she cried, doing her best to get me in the side of the head with the surprisingly hard crusty loaf.

Another woman climbed into the bus carrying a cooler box full of sweating drinks in one hand, and a tray of unlikely confectionery in the other. I bought a bottle of green liniment for my inevitable headache, along with a packet of Mentos and a can of Red Bull. Naturally she overcharged me wildly, and though the whole transaction had been conducted in Vietnamese she went on to have a long chat with the bus driver's wife about how she'd overcharged me on account of my being a foreigner. This caused the bus driver's wife to embark on a long reflection about how she should have charged me for three seats rather than two, and to wonder if perhaps it wasn't too late to insist on such a change. And all the while I could feel the steady beat, beat, beat of a baguette against the side of my neck. Ten minutes had elapsed, and still no sign of us leaving.

After the appointed time for our departure had itself long departed, the bus driver's wife gave the nod and our little mini-bus made a stately exit through the boom gates of the station, the official on duty carefully noting the bus's registration plate and our time of departure. Cordial greetings were given all around. The bus pulled onto the main road on its way to Tay Ninh, and almost immediately pulled over and opened its doors, dozens of people spilling in. All had luggage and were on their way to Tay Ninh and a brisk trade in fares was being conducted, though the tickets were not reduced in price in any way. It seemed as though the people waiting on the street outside the station simply wanted to bypass the bothersome official process of being issued with a paper ticket, or perhaps didn't want to be wearied by walking the 100 metres into the bus station itself.

There were also about half a dozen young ruffians who tumbled onto the bus clutching more baskets of baguettes to sell. The moment they saw me they gave up any pretence of shifting their wares, and instead all sat around and annoyed me with foolish questions and impertinent observations about my physical appearance.

Once the bus was pretty much loaded up, the wife gave a call and we sped off, most of the baguette boys leaping from the side door but some staying to sit next to me in order to entertain themselves further. 'Shouldn't you get off?' I enquired. 'The bus is leaving now.' The boys all scoffed at my naïveté.

'A few more rounds yet, my friend,' they laughed. 'We'll have plenty of time to get off.' And indeed, the bus did a U-turn at the roundabout and headed down the other side of the road outside the station, pulling in for its second collection of passengers, produce and hawkers. This time we had become dangerously crowded, and when one of the boys leapt on the bus shouting, 'Police! Quick, drive off!', I thought we might at last be headed for our destination.

But no. Another U-turn and we were once again driving up the street, right past the boom gates and the station officials who had noted our details. They even waved. We pulled over once more and the bus driver's wife got off and ordered a coffee from a roadside stall, shouting out to passers-by, 'Bus to Tay Ninh! Off to Tay Ninh now! Last chance to Tay Ninh!' Barely had she bolted down a condensed-milk coffee when she let out a scream and threw her substantial form onto the bus. 'Police!' she called to her husband behind the wheel. 'Drive! Now! Mother-fuckers. Haven't they got something better to do than harass a woman trying to earn a living?'

The baguette boys explained that the police were trying

to crack down on the illegal collection of passengers from the streets outside the bus station. Naturally, the drivers and their spouses saw this all as a game, and all they did was circle the station again and again till they felt they had maximised the profit-making potential of their trip. The hawkers, especially the agile young baguette boys, acted as lookouts, running screaming down the crowded streets warning the drivers. In return, they were permitted unfettered access to their captive passengers.

After the third lap, it was decided that we should hit the high road and actually set forth for Tay Ninh. We made our way painfully slowly through the outskirts of the city. All the while the bus driver's wife hung her head and arm out the window crying, '*Tay Ninh day! Tay Ninh oi!*' as she beat the side of the minibus in the hope of gathering in a few more paying customers.

CAO DAI

Despite its relentless visual bizarreness of disembodied eyes and day-glo dragons, the whole experience of Cao Dai can be surprisingly moving. As a religion, its central notions of the oneness of humanity and the unity of all religions are praiseworthy. There is something about its rococo excess that comforts the modern mind. How can you dislike a religion that is so indiscriminate in its use of colour? The massive cathedral of the Cao Dai Holy See in Tay Ninh is a visual riot, with its papier-mache dragons descending down pink plaster columns, holding up a vaulted ceiling painted like the sky itself. The cathedral is, in fact, a recreation of the universe, and the Cao Dai sacred texts speak of a world about to recreate itself.

At prayer times the cathedral fills with the white-robed devotees. Mountains of shoes are left outside, and the devout busy themselves directing and organising the tourists, cleaning the surrounds, supervising the traffic. The Cao Dai faithful seem to be inveterate organisers, which is perhaps the great strength of their religion.

Not once did I meet anyone who wasn't Cao Dai, and in a city of approximately one million people I think that's kind of extraordinary. These days the Tay Ninh Caodaists are a pretty laid-back bunch. The army is long gone, multiple generations have grown up within the religion, which started back in 1926, and several breakaway sects now act in opposition to the Tay Ninh orthodoxy. There is something quaintly jazz age about a religion that was founded by a group of spiritualists playing around with a planchette, and the elevated presence of Charlie Chaplin is a hint as to the potentially archaic nature of some of its doctrine.

The Cao Dai religion, in its generous efforts at inclusivity, managed to create an extraordinary pantheon of saints whose lives spoke to the modern world. Victor Hugo, Sun Yat Sen, Jesus, Buddha, the Virgin Mary—all of them, along with the aforementioned Chaplin, served as exemplars to the Cao Dai faithful of sacred living and holy aspiration. The Holy See is dotted with different chapels and prayer halls dedicated to different aspects of the divine, and devotees take their prescribed daily prayers at whichever chapel they feel a special affinity with. Linh favoured the Hall of the Feminine Divine which, in its own abstract way, celebrated the qualities embodied in the Buddhist Goddess of Mercy, along with the Taoist Empress of Heaven, the Madonna and Joan of Arc.

Away from its sacred heart, Tay Ninh is a bustling little

city. It is surprisingly clean and well-ordered. Perhaps there is something in the cultic mind that creates order. In the bad old days of old-fashioned Marxist hostility to religion, the scope of the Cao Dai Holy See was much reduced. The Caodaists had distinguished themselves under the old regime by being virulently anti-communist, and I suppose the Party needed to exact some kind of revenge. But short of destroying the entire city and banishing its inhabitants, it was always going to be impossible to eradicate Cao Dai as a religious force.

There is still, however, something cultish about the Cao Dai Holy Cathedral, particularly if you approach it, as almost all tourists do, at the time of midday prayers. The carnival-esque structure shimmers in the heat. The devotees press into the holy main hall. Laypeople dress in white robes and black turbans while the ordained sit further along in front, robed variously in red, blue or yellow to indicate the branch of the sect to which they are assigned, according to their karmic inheritance. A large orchestra and choir take up a gallery at the back of the cathedral and, unless one is at home with unfamiliar cacophonies, it is hard not to take umbrage at the extraordinary sounds that issue forth from there.

Tourists crowd the galleries that run along the top of the prayer hall, balanced on the narrow concrete walkways that were built who-knows-when and according to no known building standards code. My Vietnamese mother-in-law has several times banned me from ever climbing up onto that gallery, convinced that the whole structure is a death trap.

Most tourists can only bear the heat, noise and crowds for

fifteen minutes or so, and then they are back down the deadly, uneven stairs and into their air-conditioned tour bus, hankering for an overdue lunch. On previous visits that is exactly what I had done, leaning dangerously over the balcony to get some excellent 'local colour' shots; just type 'Cao Dai' into Google image search and see how many hundreds of tourists have done the same. But being here with Linh meant that I had greater social commitments. I couldn't swan out halfway through the service in search of a beer. As the tourists began to thin out, we both crept forward along the viewing gallery until we had come as far as we could. The too-holy section of the gallery was cordoned off by a devotee who sat cross-legged, blocking all further access. Until we reached that point I'd been wondering what the tourists kept tripping over. Personally I felt a velvet rope would have done the trick just as well, but who am I to question Vietnamese ways?

Linh, already feeling guilty for turning up to midday devotions in mufti (a Caodaist at prayer is meant to be properly clothed in ceremonial garb), fell to his knees and began whispering the liturgy. He urged me to do the same, leaning across to ask softly, 'Can you catch the words?'

'No,' I confessed. The poetic prayers and songs were variously sung and chanted, which meant I had almost no chance of keeping up with what was going on.

'The words are so beautiful,' said Linh, a tear rolling down his cheek. 'My dream is that one day you will understand them. Then you will know the power of Cao Dai.'

I was genuinely moved by this. Like almost every other writer who has visited Tay Ninh, I had been so quick to dismiss

Cao Dai as a quaint historical oddity. But here was a hardened, streetwise young man down on his knees sobbing at the power of Cao Dai's sacred words. It was obviously not something to be laughed at.

There were no tourists in the hall now, just the devotees, and Linh and I high up in the galleries. An exquisite high-pitched bell sounded and all fell silent. The instruments stopped, and the choir sang their last. Everyone brought their hands to their foreheads and created a mudra, a symbolic meditative hand gesture, while the high priest shuffled slowly up to the vast papier-mache globe that served as the centrepiece of the cathedral's altar, the huge, all-seeing eye of Cao Dai looking out from its centre. The priest walked silently around the globe while complete stillness reigned in the hall, despite the presence of hundreds of worshippers. The silence seemed to expand into the hot afternoon, and it was impossible to tell how long it lasted—a minute, five minutes, ten?

And then the old priest began to sing. All alone, in a soft and high-pitched wail. His voice reedy, but utterly beautiful. The crowd fell as one into a full bow, their foreheads touching the floor and the palms of their hands facing upwards. Linh, too, in tight jeans and a rip-off DKNY t-shirt, did the same, unobserved in the galleries. The bell sounded again, and another moment's silence. The quiet devotion of this carefully united group was worlds apart from my own spiritual experience, and yet I was included. We were a crowd, but at this moment each of us was utterly alone in our devotion. The priest called once more and the congregation rose—first the noise of their robes ruffling, and then the almost deafening sound of their combined prayers, filling the space that silence had created.

DRESSING UP

In a few short weeks it would be Tet, the lunar New Year. In Vietnam it is a holiday of enormous consequence—think of Christmas and multiply it by twelve. In the weeks leading up to Tet, people talk of it constantly. Many plan to return home to see their families for a few days and consequently work and save madly in an effort to make something of a splash when they get back to their village. Houses are repainted, debts are paid off. It is important to start the year with a clean slate, and a clean house filled with nice things and lots of lovely food. If at all possible, new clothes should be worn for at least a couple of days. Linh mentioned casually that this, for him, would be a very dire Tet indeed. 'Why?' I enquired.

'Oh, I have no new clothes—I'll be welcoming the year in my dirty old things. Very unlucky for me.'

'But you don't have any dirty old things—you're always impeccably dressed. You have an incredible wardrobe.'

Linh looked at me sadly. 'No,' he said. 'Just old jeans and shirts that I have worn all year. I don't know how I will face my family.'

'Well,' I said, taking the rather unsubtle hint, 'maybe I could buy you some new jeans . . .'

'Excellent idea,' said Linh, leaping to his feet with his motorcycle keys to the ready. 'It's a shame we are not in Saigon—we could have got something really good there. But Tay Ninh will have to do.' And so we went on a shopping frenzy, stopping at markets and boutiques and the ubiquitous Vietnamese clothing chains with names like Blue, Ninomax and BT 2000. Clothes are very cheap in Vietnam, and soon we were weighed down with the very latest in jeans and fake designer shirts, pseudo Calvin Klein underwear and a pair of Dior sunglasses that I'm almost certain Dior had nothing to do with. The eight-dollar price tag might have given the game away.

'Actually,' I said, 'where does it say that for the New Year you need new sunglasses?'

'You want me to get wrinkles at Tet?' asked Linh, outraged.

We rode past groups of little old ladies dressed in simple white robes on their way to prayers at the Holy Cathedral and nearly knocked them over with the bulging shopping bags draped all over the motorcycle.

'You seem pretty well set up for Tet now,' I said. 'I thought Caodaists were only meant to wear white anyhow?'

'You're living in the past,' said Linh. 'I am a *modern* Caodaist. Clothes are important.'

To get back to his house we had to drive right through the Citadel, and the elder priests were walking up to the prayer halls, dressed elaborately and exquisitely in silken robes of the brightest red, yellow and blue, their brocaded mitres stretching to the sky. The riotous colour of the cathedral building itself was rendered almost beautiful in the setting sun. I realised that, like most religions, Cao Dai was excessively concerned with matters of aesthetics. On the way to eternity, it was important to make something of a sartorial splash. Linh was right. When it came to matters of the spirit, clothes *were* important.

OFF TO SEE
THE BLACK LADY

had attempted many times to visit the Black Lady Mountain, but each and every attempt had been thwarted. For years the mountain sat there, taunting me with its squat solitude. It is the only other thing in Tay Ninh, apart from the legendary supermarket and the Cao Dai Holy City. I asked Linh to take me out there on a boiling hot Monday afternoon, and he leapt at the chance. For him the *Nui Ba Den* meant only two things: fun park and cable car.

On our way up to the mountain, strolling past closed refreshment stalls, an odd little man came running up breathlessly behind us. 'Friends!' he said. 'I'm so glad I've caught up with you. I wanted to save you all the trouble. You see, the mountain's closed today. No cable car at all on a Monday!' Linh looked crestfallen, and I was momentarily shaken—the famous shrine to the Black Lady was about to elude me again. But then our little messenger went on.

'Fortunately, there is something I can offer you as an alternative. If you just follow me, there is a small temple. I know the abbott. He can tell your fortune and work out just about any problem you have. You need only make a small offering.' Naturally I scoffed, but Linh was drawn in—I never ceased to be amazed by the credulity of the Vietnamese, trained from the cradle to believe anything stated with sufficient authority.

'No,' I said. 'I think we'd rather just walk around the mountain and take in the sights.'

'What sights?' cried the small fellow. 'Nothing to see here, brothers. Only thing you'll catch sight of on a Monday afternoon is brigands and maybe some mountain ghosts.' At this Linh turned to me with a worried look.

'Mountain ghosts?' he mouthed, his eyes wide. Anything was possible; this was, after all, Nui Ba Den, the Black Lady Mountain.

'Come with me, little brothers—I'll take care of you.' He took us by the elbows, but I shook him off and made my way further up the mountain path. Linh stood between us, his loyalties torn. 'Crazy foreigners!' cried the little man. 'Do what you like, but don't say I didn't warn you.'

Linh ran to catch up to me. 'Why were you so rude to that man?' he asked. 'He was telling us the truth. There are mountain ghosts everywhere.'

I snorted. 'He was lying,' I said. 'Can't you see he was trying to scam us?'

'Oh, I don't think so. I think we should go. He said that

everything is closed and look,' he said, gesturing toward a boarded-up restaurant, 'he seems to be right.'

I had to admit things did look a little sleepy, but my pride was hurt and I walked on ahead in a huff. The mountain drew me to it, and I knew that it had been a sacred object of devotion since the dawn of time. I suspected it was the true source of much of the famous Tay Ninh mysticism. Coming around a corner, we were greeted with the sight of the cable car gliding slowly up the mountain side, each car filled with giggling couples or families with small children. I turned to Linh and smirked triumphantly. 'How did you know?' he asked.

I was rather grateful for the cable car, because in the heat of the afternoon a spot of brisk mountain climbing was the last thing I felt like. When we reached the top I noticed several temples and shrines crowding the summit. This holy mountain had always been at turns feared and revered for its mystical power.

'Which is Ba Den, the Black Lady shrine?' I asked.

I noticed an unusual number of tiny young men wandering about the temple complex. They were not children, indeed they were quite strong-looking and many of them were heavily tattooed. But they were all quite tiny, much smaller than the average Vietnamese and, it seemed to me, bordering on dwarves. They were dressed improbably in trendy jeans and the shimmery tight t-shirts that Vietnamese men usually wear to dance clubs. They smiled at me whenever they walked past, and all seemed to be engaged as temple workers.

The biggest temple was a Buddhist one, populated by nuns and dedicated to Kwan Yin, the Buddhist Goddess of Mercy. A huge statue of Kwan Yin stood outside this temple, dressed elaborately in a red velour cloak. Her neck was hung in hundreds of beads and cheap necklaces. All this finery had been donated by pilgrims who had had their prayers answered. Each season, supplicants to the Goddess vied to supply her with her ornate cloak. Such acts of devotion also occurred in the cities, wherever there was a statue of a bodhisattva thought particularly good at answering prayers.

A bodhisattva is a perfect, enlightened being who has renounced the benefits of nirvana and chosen to be reborn into the world in order to continue to help and enlighten human beings. It is the bodhisattvas who so clutter up the average Buddhist temple. The most famous bodhisattva is of course Kwan Yin.

But the original Black Lady was still there, in a much smaller shrine to the left of the Buddhist temple. She was attended by her own community, nuns too, but these ones were devotees of the Ba Den only. They endlessly swept and washed the tiny shrine building, and directed pilgrims to the main altar in a tiled cave. The statue of the Black Lady sat on a natural rock shelf. As all such objects of devotion tend to be, she was rather unremarkable. A simple antique statue, stained a dark brown from decades of incense, here was the legendary spirit who inhabited the mountain and whose mystic energy managed to infect everyone on the plains surrounding her. I dropped to my knees in respect; I was now the only pilgrim in the shrine room, which had been packed with bodies when I first squeezed in. A tiny old nun who looked to be about 100 years old sat on a high chair, sounding the enormous old bell at intervals, its rings reverberating through the little cave. I reached into my pocket and took out my wallet, wanting to leave a modest donation at this remarkable place. Just as I was about to slide my note into the locked donation box, the ancient nun called out. 'Here!' she said. 'Leave the money with me.' I dutifully handed it over, and in return she gave me an expired lottery ticket which she had folded into a paper crane, along with two little mandarins. Later, when I ate them, they were hard and bitter.

Linh had stayed outside and was now negotiating the purchase of a serious quantity of lottery tickets from one of the dozens of panhandlers who had been harassing us since we arrived. I thought that perhaps his own Cao Dai beliefs had stopped him from paying his respects at the shrine. He told me this wasn't the case. 'I'm just scared of the Black Lady,' he said. 'I don't want to go into that cave.' The very short, bright-eyed woman selling him the lottery tickets turned her attention to me.

'Buy a ticket, fatty,' she urged. 'Lots of luck on the Nui Ba Den. No need to be afraid like your friend here.'

I noticed some more shrines just over the hill, across a ravine. 'What are those?' I asked. 'Can we go and see them?' Linh assented, apprehensively.

There was a short path running down into the ravine, and at the bottom of it a paved area. This seemed to house a camp of the small workers. The men were sitting shirtless, throwing back beers, and the equally tiny women were cooking over an open fire. They were all very jolly; their eyes sparkled and they seemed to be quite beautiful. Obviously this was the living quarters of all the temple attendants I'd been seeing about the place. Where they all from the same family? They were all short and remarkably healthy looking.

Linh grabbed at my arm and pulled me back violently. 'No,' he whispered. 'We can't go down into there. I am scared of those people.'

'But they are all so friendly,' I said. 'I don't think there's any problem. I really want to see that temple.' I pointed across to the beautiful old building, its walls washed a dusky pink.

'No,' insisted Linh. 'It's their temple. They will charge us to visit it.'

I recognised that this was a distinct possibility. Before, while visiting out of the way areas, I had been accosted by locals demanding that I pay them to visit places that I knew had no entry fee. Sometimes such encounters could grow ugly, with whole neighbourhoods gathering around demanding I pay up. This had happened in the slums on the outskirts of Ho Chi Minh City when I tried to visit a small shrine at the end of a long and densely populated alleyway. It was an experience I didn't want to repeat, so I gave in to Linh's urgings and turned back. The little people all called out after us, 'Come back, brothers! Come and have a beer with us!'

When we were out of sight, Linh stopped to sit down on a rock. 'Those people,' he said, 'they are not really people at all. They are fairies—mountain fairies. They live in the caves. They used to be people, but now they have changed . . .'

Instead of ridiculing him, I felt a little shiver pass through me. They *were* all tiny and perfectly formed, their eyes all twinkled brightly, and their teeth shone white in their smiling, chirpy faces. I *had*, for a moment, thought to myself how like elves they were.

'It is the mountain springs,' explained Linh. 'They are

magical. To drink from them once or twice is okay—it can improve your health. But some people become addicted. They come back again and again, and the spring water makes them immortal. They never return to Tay Ninh—they become fairies.'

I wanted to go back to talk to them, but Linh was insistent. 'No!' he said. 'We must go down from this mountain, I am scared.'

Pausing at the spring, I took a tumbler full of water and drank it down. Then I took another, and poured the beautifully cold and clean water all over my head. 'There,' I said, 'maybe now I will live forever.'

'Don't joke about these things,' said Linh. 'The mountain is a strange place. You don't understand. That is why we have Cao Dai—to stop the mountain's influence. Otherwise the people of Tay Ninh go crazy from the mountain.'

Just before we boarded the cable car to make our descent, Linh hunted around in his pockets. Finding the fistful of lottery tickets he had bought from the fairy woman, he checked them carefully.

'Just as I thought!' he said, thrusting a ticket into my face. 'Do you see? The date has expired. When I bought them I checked all the dates carefully, and they were fine. That is her magic—she can make the dates seem different.' Now I was spooked. I thought of the little origami lottery ticket the tiny old nun had given me, and how she had given it only to me when we were alone in the shrine room. More mountain fairy magic?

Linh dumped the tickets into the bin. 'Leave!' he cried. 'We go now!'

Coming down in our cable car, I heard crazy, high-pitched laughter coming up from the mountain beneath us. There was one of the little men, in his Hong Kong import jeans and silver polyester disco shirt. 'Bye!' he cried out manically in English. 'See you again!'

'Don't look,' begged Linh, taking my hand. 'Please, just don't look down at that fairy.'

FENG SHUI AND FLOWER ARRANGING

American Catholic bishop Fulton Sheen famously said that by following our religious impulses we gain nothing but a sense of our own littleness. It is certainly true that humility is a quality that marks almost all of the Buddhist monks and nuns I have known in Vietnam.

At first sight, the monk's life is one of the most fundamental denial of pleasure and comfort and the basics of human relationships. The monk leaves his home forever, never to experience again his mother's affection, nor the touch of a lover. No meat, no beer and rising every morning at four. Such a life seems utterly repugnant to those of us brought up in the material comforts of the West. And yet, in my experience, monastic life is lived richly and in genuine warmth and delight. There is much kindness, and while pleasures are normally heartfelt and simple they are nonetheless pleasurable. In

Vietnam the monks also inhabit a world of ritual with an easy relationship with the supernatural. As a matter of course they pray for ghosts and spirits, leaving aside a portion of their rice to feed those lost souls destined to wander the earth in desperate hunger. The monk's concern is for *all* life—not just the lives of the good or the deserving or those closely related to him. A monk prays not for his own mother, but for all mothers.

There is no doubt that monks live in a kind of parallel universe, where things can take as long as they like and where everyday commitments to the world count for little in a lifetime of sacrifice and spiritual practice. Monks are inclined to telephone excitedly and arrange an outing, only to not turn up at the agreed time. When questioned they have a tendency to look surprised at any annoyance and give a perfectly irrefutable answer, like: 'But Brother Ba had to attend a funeral and he had no money for the bus!'

I soon learned that they had exquisite ways of spending their free time. At the Zen Institute in Saigon's District 3, scores of impressively fit young monks practise martial arts on the rooftop as the sun goes down. These are stern youngsters, their shirtless torsos rippling with muscle as they quietly go through their training regimen—just the occasional flutter of their baggy pyjama bottoms as one of them flies through the air. While it all seems very Zen, the institute stands directly across an endlessly busy road from Vinh Nghiem pagoda, one of Ho Chi Minh City's premier tourist destinations.

Ho Chi Minh City, as we know it, is an invention of the Communist administrators who took over in 1975. They amalgamated the glamorous, decadent old Saigon with the outlying districts, as well as the satellite towns of Gia Dinh and Cholon. Throw in the vast districts of Thu Duc, Cu Chi and Binh Chanh, small states encompassing hundreds of farming villages, and you have the heaving mass of Ho Chi Minh City. It's a city so large and comically diverse that efficient functioning is almost impossible. Infrastructure projects stretch out over years, and those who live in the rather prosaically named Districts 1, 2, 3, 4, etcetera, doubtlessly dream of a slightly more romantic designation.

Some of the monks at the Zen Institute in District 3 are of a more bookish turn, and they spend their few leisure hours painstakingly translating books from English into Vietnamese with the aid of a cover-less communal dictionary with several key pages missing. Other monks, gentler still, indulge in flower arranging. When I first visited the institute I met a tall, thin and extremely camp monk from Quy Nhon. Brother Hien was the institute's resident interior decorator and feng shui expert, and was regularly called upon to rearrange a brother monk's cell if things weren't working out. I adored Hien. He was also an expert cook and a dab hand at massage, and his high-cheekboned face was ethereally beautiful. He always carried a fan, which he wielded with all the skill of a drag queen. It could be flicked open before giggling to cover an unbecoming laughing mouth, or folded to be used to great effect to drive home a point. Once we were chatting in his cell and one of the martial monks walked in, fresh from a practice session. Hien grimaced, took up his fan and slapped the monk on his over-inflated chest.

'I won't have naked men in my room!' he shouted, much to the amusement of all the other monks in the wing.

When I mentioned how much I admired Brother Hien, one of the martial monks answered, 'Hien is a good monk.' Then, fixing me with his sternest look, he said, 'But too womanly.'

Becoming a monk is an ancient calling that comes with more than its fair share of cultural trappings. Monks live in community, sharing their lives with people who are frequently of incompatible temperament. But in general their affectionate regard for their brothers' eccentricities overcomes petty annoyances. And once again, the Vietnamese capacity for frank and open acknowledgement of people's foibles can serve as an effective way to manage these relationships in close-knit, frequently overcrowded conditions. 'This is Brother Manh,' they will say. 'He is fat and has a tendency to oversleep.' Fault identified, person forewarned, no-one need be disappointed.

THE FURNITURE-BREAKING DEMON

In Saigon I wake too late to feasibly get to temple in the mornings, especially when one takes into account a long breakfast out. This is a non-negotiable in Vietnam, where no-one takes breakfast at home. And then there's a cup of coffee or two at a café afterwards, another non-negotiable. These may well be bad habits introduced by the French but, without the coffee, I suspect that they were in place a thousand years before Europeans ever saw Vietnam.

Kien, my Ho Chi Minh City best friend and protector, keeps his busy hairdressing salon open till late at night. I rely on him to take me out to breakfast and so I am somewhat hostage to his schedule, as he hates getting up early. Breakfast by myself was fairly unsatisfying as, being too scared to drive my own motorcycle, I was confined to the several small eateries close to my house. Most of these I had ruled out because the food was not tasty or it made me sick, as they were streetside stalls where refrigeration is unknown and hygiene was a secondary concern.

One of the places I liked to venture to on my own was the *banh cuon* shop on Pham Van Hai. *Banh cuon* is a delicious Vietnamese breakfast of fat rice noodles stuffed with a mixture of pork mince and mushroom, and steamed. These divine noodles are covered in a sweet, spicy fish sauce, and the whole meal can be eaten quite quickly and is insanely cheap.

The shop on Pham Van Hai started as a streetside stall, and I had been a customer since its earliest days. The woman who owned it cooked the *banh cuon*, while her husband attended to the customers. The tiny shop itself was minimalist, but they had invested in a large, elaborately decorated menu board. This was always entirely empty, which made sense because they only served one dish—steamed *banh cuon*. The shop owner always made a great deal of fuss over how fat I'd become whenever she saw me. 'It's not healthy,' she'd call out if I should happen to be passing down the street. 'You must get very tired. Reduce!' Whenever I stopped in for breakfast an elaborate charade always took place in which multiple plastic stools were stacked, one on top of another, so that I might have a safe seat. This was always observed with great merriment by the other customers, who pointed me out to their children and said things like, 'Look! The fat foreigner breaks the furniture. Better behave, or he'll eat you.' The excessive use of multiple pieces of furniture was probably quite sensible, given my track record. Still and all, it was humiliating.

The other breakfast option was always the Pham Ngu Lao

district, Ho Chi Minh City's backpacker paradise in District 1. Here you can eat cheesy croques-monsieur, banana pancakes and even muesli, a dish the Vietnamese look upon with singular revulsion. But you also have to run the gauntlet of rapacious street vendors, beggars and other hustlers. It even has roving teams of fake Buddhist monks and nuns who hassle tourists for cash. These dodgy characters give Buddhism a bad name. I wish that Vietnam carried the same harsh penalties for impersonating a monk as Thailand does, especially when you think of all the honest nuns and monks in the city who lead quiet lives of hard work, poverty and humility. Never give money to monks begging on the streets of central Saigon. Save it for a quiet donation at the suburban temples instead.

Many monks in Ho Chi Minh City end up learning about the building trade as quantities of able-bodied young religious are recruited from the provinces to be builders' labourers in temples. Some Buddhists have questioned the religious propriety of such practices, not to mention the morality of employing what is little more than a slave labour force.

Casual building practices mean that rooms and accommodation wings in temples are tucked into odd places, at bizarre angles or on uneven levels. The Central Monastery in District 6, one of the many monasteries in Ho Chi Minh City that bear that name, features a fourth floor, as well as floor four and a half, and a separate floor four B. And just to keep things interesting, all are accessed from completely separate parts of the monastery complex. It's wildly impractical and possibly dangerous, but the resulting hidden alcoves and secret-walled shrines make the place intriguing. I don't think even the abbott is aware of who is under his roof on any given night.

Back in 1999, the monks had invited my elderly grandparents to a meal at the monastery and they went to an inordinate amount of trouble for the visit of two unimportant septuagenarians from the West. They prepared an exquisite banquet for them, and the mahogany table reserved for guests was groaning with the most wonderful dishes: delicate *banh xeo*, mung bean pancakes coloured with saffron, and plates of Hue-style *goi cuon,* little parcels of noodles and cooked vegetables wrapped in rice paper and dipped into hoi sin. Several novices buzzed around serving us and ladled out bowls of the sweet, tamarind-flavoured soup called *canh chua.*

Suddenly and alarmingly, my poor old grandfather stood up and ran from the table. We all looked at each other, worried, and the abbott commanded me sharply, 'Go and attend to your grandfather.'

The dear old thing was out in the temple courtyard throwing up into a large bonsai pot. 'What's wrong?' I asked, rubbing his back.

He was surrounded by a small group of worried young monks. 'Should we call a doctor?' they asked. 'An ambulance?'

My grandfather, a solid, country man, was not the sort to make a fuss. Standing up and wiping his mouth, he said, 'I'm fine. Just came over all funny for a second. Must have been the cooking oil. Perhaps it was that fish sauce.' He had lived in fear of fish sauce, the most common Vietnamese seasoning, ever since I had explained the process by which it was produced.

'Grandad,' I said, 'this is a monastery. They don't use fish sauce.'

'Buggered if I know,' he grumbled, losing his patience. 'I just feel crook.'

The monks led him into the abbott's room, and a bottle of imported *dau xanh*, the green Chinese liniment, was found. The monks began to rub it on his head and his wrists. One unbuttoned his shirt and began to apply it to his back. 'Bloody hell,' said Grandad, looking ill and ill-at-ease, 'I hope they don't take my pants off as well.'

One day my friend from the monastery took me on a day-trip to Vung Tau, a beach resort just outside of Ho Chi Minh City that once bore the infinitely more romantic name of Cap St Jacques. This is where all Saigonese, even monks, dream of going to relax. It is a longish trip, with frequently bad traffic conditions. We found ourselves arriving back at the monastery a little late, having been held up in the hellish traffic on the city's outskirts. Considering the time, my friend told me I could stay at the monastery, and a suitable place was found for me to sleep on a little terrace housing a shrine to Amitabha, the Buddha of the Western Paradise, and a great object of devotion for most Vietnamese Buddhists. The shrine was busy, with its big plaster statue of Amitabha, his hands outstretched, and a little collection of minor deities at his feet. There were fruit and flowers, and a large porcelain pot painted with Chinese characters for holding incense. It was outdoors, but a mosquito net was rigged up for me. After much fuss sorting out the direction toward which my feet should be pointed—not toward any shrines, or the abbott's room, or toward any of the monks' quarters—I settled down for the night on my breezy little veranda high up in the monastery, looking out over the city's lights. I drifted off to sleep for what must have been three hours at most. At 3.30 am the temple's novices woke up and dusted down the shrines, ready to sound the bell at four for the rest of the monks to rise.

No-one had been warned of my presence on the Amitabha terrace, so the sight of my rotund form dozing away in front of the shrine must have appeared faintly miraculous. One or two may have thought I was an apparition of Di Lac, the fat laughing Buddha of the future. I woke to find myself surrounded by giggling novices wiping down the altar and offering new sticks of incense to the Buddha. Then one of the boys reached up to the altar and plucked a persimmon from the offerings there and wordlessly handed it to me. I sat up on the cool tiles and ate it, breathing in the fresh incense smoke and listening to the dawn temple bell.

I was struck by his simple kindness, by the kindness constantly shown by people who had no reason to be interested in me or my journey. There was such a generous simplicity in this offering of food. It was a supremely human moment, a celebration of the connection of one person with another. Sitting on that freshly swept terrace with persimmon juice on my chin, I was reminded that it is almost always the small, the momentary, that is most significant. In that second your under-standing shifts, and the world is the same no longer. These little moments of realisation are added to the litany of small life-changing secrets we reflect on again and again.

FORGOTTEN ANCESTORS

Heat and traffic are the two things that constantly terrorise you in Ho Chi Minh City. As the city grows, people become more and more motorised and cars begin to encroach upon the more malleable flow of motorcycles. While the city governors continue to embark on seemingly eternal projects of streetscaping and improvement, the place becomes more and more oppressive. It is hard to get around by any method of transportation. By foot is the hardest of all.

With a population officially calculated at six million—though most think the real figure is much higher—the density of housing is truly terrifying. People live crammed down alleyways and within impossibly complex labyrinths of little streets that can barely fit a person riding a motorcycle. Front rooms open directly to the street. A trip through these back alleys will offer up endless tableaux of day-to-day life for the idly curious: shirtless old men sit on their stoops smoking and scratching the ears of ugly yellow dogs; mothers and maids hold babies out the door while they urinate into the street, or worse.

As the streets clog up, large temple compounds shrink as pieces of land are sold for housing development. One of the largest still intact is the Giac Lam temple complex out along the farther reaches of Lac Long Quan street in Ho Chi Minh City's endless suburbia. In one of the cloisters there is a large mural depicting the torments to be expected in hell. Inspired by Vietnamese and Chinese folk religion, with a touch of Buddhism, they serve as powerful moral lessons, the gory fates of the slothful and the libidinous vividly depicted in a way that must inevitably sear itself into memory. The lustful and adulterous are condemned to climb endlessly up spiked metal poles that tear at their genitals. Liars spend a lifetime having their tongues seared and pierced. One unhappy group is doomed to hop in and out of pots of boiling oil, though I couldn't quite work out what their original sin had been.

Famously, the greedy are destined to be reborn as hungry ghosts, with enormous distended bellies and only tiny pinholes for mouths. The capricious attendants of this ghastly underworld feed them delicious morsels of food, but just as they bring them to their mouths these comestibles burst into flame, burning the poor creatures' mouths and faces.

It was in this state that the enlightened bodhisattva Dia Tang, the Earth Store Bodhisattva, discovered his mother during a psychic visit to hell. He begged the Buddha to allow him to relieve her suffering, and out of compassion the Buddha relented. And so all is not lost, as Dia Tang now serves as the protector of the dead, looking out over every soul.

At Giac Lam pagoda, the old Hall of the Dead is a reasonably shabby affair. It is centuries old. Generation after generation has stored the ashes of its loved ones here, in glazed ceramic vases that now stand rows deep on the crumbling cement shelves. Dia Tang stands at the doorway, holding an iron staff with six rings suspended from its top. Each ring represents one of the Buddhist Perfections—kindness, morality, patience, persistence, attention and insight. The six rings jingle as he travels, thereby sending the sounds of the Perfections throughout the universe. And the staff itself can be used to open the gates of hell, ultimately liberating the poor souls he is charged with protecting.

Kien had brought me there to visit his paternal grandfather, a man who had died many years before. We came with offerings for Dia Tang, but more importantly we brought a cash gift for the young monk attendant who sat at a desk to the left of the shrine. Guide books will often tell you there is no tipping in Vietnam, but I have no idea where they got that notion from. The Vietnamese, if they can afford it, tip regularly. And as a foreign visitor who is indisputably wealthier than almost everyone he will encounter, I know a dollar or two I would otherwise waste at home can go a long way to extending the impossibly low wages that most people in Vietnam earn.

This monk had access to the mouldy ledgers that recorded exactly where everyone's remains were kept in the building. He disappeared to the back of the hall, and some minutes later he returned bearing a lime green ceramic vase with a photograph of the old man glazed onto it. For some more cash, the monk placed the vase on the altar with our offerings and, ordering us to our knees, he chanted a small section of the sutras, using a little hand-held bell for extra effect. We all offered incense, and Kien left well pleased with his act of filial piety. 'I always loved my *ong noi*,' he said. 'When he got really old I used to bathe him.'

It seemed that Kien's *ong noi* had been something of an old rogue. Separating from his wife in Hanoi, he had travelled south during the troubles of the mid 1950s and started a new family. By the time Kien knew him he was a wizened little man who would shuffle around the local petrol stations begging small change from the people filling up their ancient motorcycles.

At the end the old grandfather gave up bathing, then gave up eating. While the whole family barely got by on survival rations, Kien's *ong noi* decided to stop trying. Kien would try to bathe him every day, and try to feed him whatever leftovers there were, but it was already too late. The whole family was starving, and who could argue with an old and useless man who could only ever be a liability in hard times? 'It was his karma,' said Kien, his eyes filling with tears. 'He abandoned his family in the north when he was young, and so when he was old no-one could help him. That's why I like to come and see him now. Now I have money and I can buy him good things. I can get the monks to sing for him, though I never remember him going to a temple.'

In Vietnam there is a certain fatalism when it comes to assessing people's fortunes. In Le Ly Haslip's harrowing memoir of the war, *When Heaven and Earth Changed Places*, her mother explains: 'The village—the whole country—must have done something terrible for fate to punish us so much. But that's our karma. If you're lucky, you'll go to your ancestors before you have to suffer any more.'

As we stepped outside the temple gates a score of beggars set upon us, almost all impossibly old men and women, tiny and thin and dressed in rags. Having dispensed our change, Kien reflected, 'Any of these people, too, could have been my grandfather in another life. But you mustn't feel bad—they are like this because of their karma. Nothing happens by accident. You can help them if you are kind, or if you want to improve your own destiny. But never for a moment imagine that people aren't exactly where they deserve to be. Who knows, maybe one day it will be you or I doing the same thing.'

There wasn't much I could say. Kien was going through a nasty divorce, something still relatively shameful and unusual in Vietnamese society. He and his wife hated each other bitterly, and she had taken his only son away to live with her in a distant ancestral village. Was he convinced that he, too, had created his own fate? 'This is Vietnam,' he said. 'Life is hard. Not like it is for you. You can go wherever you want, do whatever you want. You are a good man, with good karma.'

We sat on the antique cement stairs that led up to the paved forecourt. High-school students sat all about us, studying and flirting with each other, seeking solitude in the quiet temple grounds. We were all in the shade of an immense Bodhi tree.

'I wish I could have had your life,' said Kien, quietly.

HELLO KITTY

When in Vietnam my own fate took me to strange places, and my days were spent diversely. That afternoon, having visited the Benedictine monastery in one of the rural districts outside Ho Chi Minh City, I was offered a ride on the back of a motorbike. 'We'll just have to stop off at my house,' my kindly saviour said, 'and get you a helmet.' The man lived in one of the nearby squatters' villages, all-Catholic settlements that had sprung up around existing churches and monasteries after the 1954 Catholic exodus from the north. He had lived in the village since he was a baby, and attended mass at the monastery. He beeped his horn outside one of the shacks and a shy teenage girl came out. 'Get your father a spare helmet,' he commanded. She ran back with a bright pink helmet emblazoned with a sequinned image of Hello Kitty that glittered in the sun.

'Here we go, Brother,' he said, passing the helmet over to me. 'It's the law now.'

No-one seemed to notice or comment on my unusual choice in safety wear. I had noticed that Vietnamese men seemed unconcerned about wearing gender-unsuitable accessories in the name of necessity. It was common to see muscled, tattooed labourers strolling down the street in women's hats, for example; plonked on, I could only assume, because a hat was needed and that was the only choice available. Every house normally has a huge pile of shoes outside it, as the Vietnamese are scrupulous about removing footwear before they enter a home. Frequently I had seen men select a pair of spangly sandals or some pastel pink Mary Janes from the pile when they had to get somewhere in a hurry. I actually admired this masculine confidence. Certainly most Western men of my acquaintance, gay and straight, would absolutely refuse to wear a Hello Kitty safety helmet down a busy highway, let alone willingly saunter down to the shops in a pair of acid-green flip-flops with pom-poms on top.

My driver was an ardent Catholic, and had assumed that I was one too. 'I have heard about you,' he said. 'You are always at the monastery. People say you are a good man, a real Catholic.' I didn't know what to say to this. I hated to disappoint him by going into detail about my Protestant family and interfaith leanings. So I took the coward's way out and remained silent.

'I imagine,' he said, 'that you are going to attend the feast of Fatima? That's a biggie around here. Miracles galore, and everyone gets dressed up and parades around the street. And La Vang! Have you visited La Vang yet?'

'What is La Vang?' I asked.

'You don't know La Vang? Little Brother, you must get there as soon as you can!' He was becoming quite excited, turning his head to me in order to chat more easily, though we continued to weave in between and in front of enormous trucks on the highway. 'La Vang,' he shouted against the wind, 'is the home of the Blessed Virgin Mary in Vietnam. It is where the Holy Mother appears in the forest. You have to go to La Vang!'

My curiosity obviously excited, he told me about Our Lady of La Vang all the way on the long trip home. I got him to drop me off in front of Kien's salon. I wondered why the apprentices were all staring at me—seeing me dismount from some ramshackle old motorcycle all dusty and windswept was almost an everyday occurrence by now, and they normally ignored me completely.

'What was with the helmet?' asked Kien when I came inside. 'Did you really wear that thing all the way from Thu Duc? You looked like a freak.'

'I don't care,' I said, 'I am going to see the Virgin Mary in La Vang.'

'La Vang?' snorted Kien. 'You'll be killed. The place is filled with religious maniacs. Very far, and very dangerous. Please don't go there.'

But I had made up my mind. The Blessed Virgin was calling me.

TATTOOED DRAGON

A sking around Catholic friends, I discovered that La Vang, the site of visions of the Virgin Mary, was in Quang Tri, a province adjoining Hue, right in the centre of Vietnam. As it happened I had a friend in Quang Tri, a man called Ly who I'd known in Ho Chi Minh City and who had recently moved back to his home village because, as he said, he missed his mother. I suspected other, less filial motivations. In Saigon, Ly led something of a shadow life. A drinker and a gambler, in recent years he had become a small-time gangster, fulfilling mysterious roles at billiard halls and 'restaurants' that kept unusually late hours and seemed to boast of inordinate numbers of beautiful young 'waitresses'. Ly was a sad and angry young man, a fatherless child who had come to Saigon to improve his lot and had succeeded only in getting lost in its sometimes terrifying underbelly.

I had often wondered how Ly's reception back home had gone. During his years in Ho Chi Minh City he had acquired a number of things. A slender but dark scar ran from his temple across his high cheekbone, and his knuckles bore tattoos that declared how sad he was about his life. From his neck to his waist, a huge, multicoloured dragon twisted around his body, a truly impressive piece of skin art that had cost him a small fortune and many hours of pain. He was hardly the image of a local boy made good. But something about Ly had always shone above his life and circumstances. As bad as he undoubtedly was he still carried within him a great desire to be good, possibly to be the strong, honest and kind boy his lonely mother doubtless believed him to be.

When I called and told him I would soon be arriving in Hue, Ly was terribly excited and promised to travel to Hue from his home town to meet me at the airport. Whenever he spoke to me he used the exaggeratedly polite language that a student would use with his teacher. This meant that conversations with him could be unnecessarily long and complicated, filled with florid expressions of respect and subservience. In the same way that he would try to cover the tattoos on his knuckles whenever we met, or wear buttoned-up shirts to disguise the dragon's talons that clawed up his neck, Ly used the language of a well-mannered schoolboy to try to impress on me that, no matter what others might say, he was a good person, deserving of my friendship.

For some reason my flight to Hue was delayed, not by one or two hours, but by six. This being Vietnam no explanation was given, but the slightly arrogant young woman attending the check-in counter kindly gave me a lunch voucher to be redeemed at the airport cafeteria. Naturally, when I went to use the voucher I discovered that none of the free lunch options was actually available, so I paid instead for a Red Bull and a stale little sponge cake filled with green bean paste. I was very, very grumpy, and the hard plastic chairs of Ho Chi Minh City domestic airport were no place to spend six hours of enforced leisure.

I called Ly and explained my predicament, and he seemed to understand the situation. But then, every forty minutes or so he began calling me. 'Are you here yet?' he would ask.

'Ah, no—I told you, the plane is delayed by six hours. I won't be there till the late afternoon. There's no need to meet me at the airport. We'll meet in Hue for a drink tonight.'

'*Da*, excellent idea, Older Brother,' replied Ly with his comically exaggerated politesse.

Then, an hour later, he called again. Each time with the same question, each time the same response. Did he think I was lying to him? Or perhaps he thought I was secretly in Hue, avoiding him. I had noticed that each time he called the question became more and more slurred, his response more emotional, more unnecessarily polite. I guessed that he was killing time at one of Hue's cheap alfresco wine bars—the little plastic tables and stools that housewives set up on the foot-path and from which they dispensed home-distilled rice spirits from big plastic jars, each jar boasting some special addition to flavour the spirit. Some jars featured hands of green bananas suspended in the alcohol, others had medicinal herbs. The more expensive ones boasted the flavour of field rat, turtle or snake, the animal's corpse just visible in the cloudy liquid.

I finally got to Hue and found my adorable little hotel on Chu Van An street. Foreigners invariably love Hue, jammed full as it is of history and crumbling ruins, ancient temples and palaces, and tombs situated along the Perfume River in the middle of nowhere, far from all settlement. The old Imperial City that stands at the centre of Hue, though humble by world standards, is still charming and surprisingly well-preserved.

While I was checking into my hotel, Ly called again. 'Big Brother *oi*!' he cried. It sounded as though he were at a night-club, or at least in the midst of a very noisy party. He was slurring so much he was almost incomprehensible. 'Where are you?' I told him I was at the hotel, and he promised he would be right by to see me. After my ghastly day sitting around the airport I was in a foul mood, and not at all inclined to see people or entertain. I had decided on an early night, perhaps even eating at the hotel restaurant, the ultimate sin of slothful-ness for the traveller. But I also knew that once someone in Vietnam had decided on seeing you, it was impossible to say no. In fact, it was infinitely easier to say yes and then try to end the social interaction as early as possible, claiming fatigue or illness.

'I have a friend coming to see me,' I told the woman behind the counter.

'Oh, a *friend*,' she leered, giving me an exaggerated wink. 'One hour in Hue and you have a *friend* already. Shall I send her straight up?'

'Actually,' I said, cultivating my most prissy exterior, 'it's a man, and no, there is no need to send him up. Just call me and I will come down.'

After two hours there was still no sign of Ly, so I started to get ready to go to dinner. My room phone rang, and the woman at the front desk, sounding slightly alarmed, said, 'Sir, there's a man here who says he wants to see you.' Then, in a stage whisper, she added, 'He's drunk.'

I came down to the lobby and the minute the lift doors opened I could smell Ly. He was in front of the desk holding court with the two disapproving young women behind it. His skin blackened by the sun, his shirt unbuttoned enough to reveal the angry head of his elaborate tattooed dragon and extravagantly, swayingly drunk, Ly was not the type to inspire confidence in hotel front desk staff. The girls glared at me, and other guests stared in fascination as we greeted each other and Ly attempted to chat with me in a braying, drunkard's voice. His affected Saigonese accent and the unnecessary courtliness of his language were only exaggerated by his drunkenness. I quickly ushered him out of the hotel, but forever after that the staff seemed ever so slightly scared of me. Through association I had become a tough guy, a shadowy character who obviously knew some frighteningly disreputable people in the city. I kind of enjoyed the reputation.

LOSING HOPE
IN HUE

Ly and I walked down by the Perfume River, enjoying the cool air and the changing multicoloured lights projected onto the squat little Louis Eiffel designed bridge. Ly's dream was to study driving and acquire a delivery driver's licence. He had a friend in business delivering Huda beer across Quang Tri province, and there was always a vacancy for a good driver. I was happy about his dream, and pleased that there was something he wanted to work toward.

I offered to pay for the first round of lessons and tests, a process of unimaginable bureaucratic complexity in Vietnam. The government seemed to have something of a set against drivers of four-wheeled vehicles, and acquiring a driver's licence is both expensive and interminable. Once you have a licence you must prepare for a yearly review and renewal, a process that can involve several days of waiting at various government offices.

The piece of paper itself, along with the accompanying driving lessons, is reasonably cheap. But the bribes that must be paid to every petty bureaucrat one encounters quickly make the whole process cripplingly expensive and quite soul destroying.

A poor village boy like Ly, with an absentee father and a Year 9 education, is almost without options in modern-day Vietnam. The most he can hope for is a life driving someone else's truck. I suggested that perhaps, if he worked hard and saved his money, he could buy his own vehicle in five years or so and really start to be in control of his life. 'Don't, please don't,' he said, turning to me with deadly seriousness. 'I don't want to get carried away with dreams. One dream is enough for right now.'

This almost broke my heart, possibly because it was the kind of expectation I encountered over and over again in Vietnam. Hopes are for foreigners, the rich or people with family overseas. Or just for the extraordinarily lucky. The great bulk of the population, poorly educated and underpaid, seems to be without goals. They are intent on getting by, and are bewildered and angered by the 'economic miracle' that they hear so much about yet find so very hard to believe in.

In the West, where people plan quite legitimately for careers as television celebrities or travel writers and where 70-year-olds begin undergraduate degrees in social ecology, our dreams are constantly on the surface and always encouraged. But in Vietnam it's all too common to meet 22-year-olds who have long ago abandoned their dreams, and 50-year-olds who are retiring from active work because their bodies are just worn out. There is no sense of possibility, of that drift towards progress that we accept as the norm in the West, what Benedictine nun and cultural visionary Joan Chittister describes as 'growing into dreams at every stage of life'. For people like Ly, dreams are in short supply and need to be strictly doled out, one at a time. Failure to guard one's dreams may result in much more bitter disappointments.

In spite of this—or perhaps because of it—there's something about being in Vietnam that made me feel that anything was possible. Such a belief in my own invincibility was encouraged by the people around me, who were all equally convinced of the fact that I could do anything I wanted. Why couldn't I? I was a rich man living in a rich country with no foreseeable anxieties about where to live or how to pay for my meal. Let's face it, the life I led was already the stuff of fantasy to most people in Vietnam. Why not grasp the bull by the horns and do an apprenticeship in violin-making, then build an orphanage in Mongolia? I would convince myself that I was a free spirit, and that the days of wasting my opportunities were all over now.

Months later, when I got home and flicked through my journals, the lists I'd made of what I would do upon my return made me sad. They never said 'Gain four kilos' or 'Watch inordinate amounts of daytime television'—things I really would achieve. The lofty goals of my time away, borne of an awareness of my own privilege, were just so hard to take seriously. Sometimes I would tear them out of my journal and throw them away. Opportunity, conditions, leisure time—all of these things were still exactly the same as I imagined they would be once I got home, perhaps even more amenable. Conditions were perfect. Everything was in place, only my enthusiasm had died.

How do I explain myself in Vietnam, where most everyone I know struggles to survive, where they subsist on paltry wages and have no chance to change things because they work fourteen-hour days, seven days a week? How do I explain why I'm not rich, or famous, or in possession of my own business? That I am thirty-eight and have achieved really very little in life? To say as much would be an insult to them. So I buy into their fantasies about me, that I am someone special and extraordinary, brilliantly clever because I can string together a few childish sentences in their language and make my way clumsily through a tabloid newspaper.

I learn to think big in Vietnam, but when I get home my dreams shrink.

OUR LADY OF
LA VANG

'I want you take me to La Vang,' I said to Ly.

'I didn't know you were Catholic,' he replied.

'I'm not—it's just that someone told me about La Vang and I feel I need to see it.' Ly looked sceptical. La Vang was in his home province, and it was a place he knew well.

'You know, there's not really much to see in La Vang. It's just a village. Sometimes filled with crazy Catholics, but mostly just empty.'

But I was adamant, and he promised to call for me the next day and take me to La Vang. Being used to customary early starts I was up and about by five, but Ly didn't turn up till nine, looking red-eyed and awful. He was wearing the same clothes he'd had on the night before, and he smelled terribly of alcohol and a strong, though not yet offensive, body odour. The Vietnamese are scrupulous about showering and personal

hygiene, and cleanliness is one of their most frequent and pressing concerns. Ly's sharp, sour scent was a shock to me, but I
attributed it to the after-effects of the rice spirits and the fact
that he looked as though he had slept outdoors. 'Do you *really*
want to go to La Vang?' he asked. 'It's a dump, you know.'

We caught a taxi out to one of the highways and stopped
in the middle of nowhere. We stood there on the lonely road,
exposed to the elements, for nearly an hour till we finally
flagged down a passing minibus. 'Going to La Vang, Boss?'
asked Ly.

'We're going to Dong Ha. Get in and I'll drop you at the
La Vang turn-off—you can walk from there.' We squeezed
in—the bus was already filled to capacity, plus some. I was put
into the front seat, and Ly continued his negotiations from
the back.

'So, Uncle, how much would I have to pay you to go by
the La Vang way?'

'No can do, Little Brother. This bus takes the highway
direct to Dong Ha. You've got a fine pair of legs on you, and
the foreigner looks like a buffalo. Two strong fellows like your-
selves should have no problems walking to La Vang.' Ly didn't
respond, though I was apprehensive at the thought of trudging
down a country road in the terrible heat for who knows how
many kilometres to an unknown destination.

After some time, Ly piped up again, seemingly spontaneously.
'You know, it occurs to me that for just a few thousand dong,
you might be able to swing us by La Vang and it wouldn't add
ten minutes to your trip.' The driver seemed not to have heard
this casual observation, and kept his eyes steadily on the road.

After about ten minutes the driver said, 'A hundred thousand dong and I'll drop you at the gates.' And so, in a bus packed full of uncomplaining passengers who all thought they were headed direct to Dong Ha, our little bus turned down a muddy country lane and took a half-hour detour in order to drop me at La Vang, one of the holiest sites of pilgrimage in Vietnam.

For such a spiritually significant spot, I guess I was expecting something a little special. But getting off the bus, I stepped straight into a seeping pile of mud; La Vang is a poor village, and the streets are unpaved. The whole complex devoted to Mary was, well, a little scruffy-looking. I was beginning to feel that Ly had been right—it was a dump. Ly had a pained expression, making it obvious that he was here only to amuse me. He pulled out a cigarette as we ducked under the closed gate. 'I don't know why you Catholics want to come to such a godforsaken place,' he grumbled.

'I told you before, I'm not a Catholic.'

'Whatever,' he said, striding down the long, overgrown field that led to the bombed-out basilica, allegedly the site of the original apparitions. It was close to midday, and hot as only central Vietnam can be. Ly was headed to the shade of the basilica but I dawdled, taking photographs of the bizarre modernist statues that ran the length of the field showing various versions of the Virgin. An extremely hideous church had been built and to its left was a huge tank of holy water and a fun park–style shrine to Our Lady of La Vang. As represented in statues all over Vietnam and among Vietnamese communities abroad, Our Lady of La Vang is an elegant figure. Dressed in the traditional *ao dai* and turban of Vietnamese women of old, she represents the Virgin Mary in her oriental aspect, holding a small Vietnamese baby and reminding the world that the idea of the Christ is a truly universal one. It was in this guise that she appeared to the peasant farmers and Catholic refugees escaping persecution by the emperor and living in the jungles of La Vang in 1798.

Found in church courtyards and streetside shrines, statues of Our Lady of La Vang are genuine objects of devotion to the Vietnamese people, and the image of her is obviously deeply inspiring. She is sometimes gracefully rendered in white marble, reminding me of the classical *blanc de Chine* statuettes of the Buddhist Goddess of Mercy, Kwan Yin. But in La Vang the Virgin is rendered monumentally in cement, her vast statue rather spookily sheltered by outsized concrete mushrooms. There was nothing particularly inspiring about this shrine, and the merciless sun didn't help. What struck me was that there was absolutely no-one about. It is a reasonably large complex, and this absence of people in usually crowded Vietnam was quite unsettling. I hunted Ly down, smoking under an annexe and looking desperately bored. 'In there,' he said, pointing towards the ghastly church, 'some nuns. Saying prayers. I suppose you should go in—you'll know what's going on.'

'I probably won't,' I said. But I snuck in, and sure enough there were half a dozen chubby Vietnamese nuns in black veils conducting a prayer service with a handful of congregants. I stayed for the duration of the service, more to be out of the heat than for any other reason. The church was resolutely un-air-conditioned. This lack of air-conditioning is a point of pride for both Catholics and Buddhists in Vietnam. These days most temples and churches could probably afford to have their main buildings climate-controlled, but in a misguided quest for simplicity they refuse, preferring to see the faithful swelter and faint in the heat. It has arisen as an issue because Vietnam's Protestant churches, flush with cash from American benefactors, are plush-seated and air-conditioned, and they regularly boast about it. The Buddhists and Catholics, seeing themselves as the true representatives of the stoic Vietnamese spirit, point to such unnecessary luxury as evidence of Protestantism's unsuitability to the Vietnamese spiritual landscape.

I felt a tap on my shoulder, and turned to see it was Ly. 'I have a friend, he has a taxi,' he whispered. 'I called him and he will be here in a few minutes. *Please* can we leave now? I want to take you to see my mother.' We trudged back out to the muddy street, and a couple of terrifying dogs from the nearby houses came out to growl and snap at me. Dogs in Vietnam's rural areas despise foreigners, I had noticed. Out of nowhere a motley crew of beggars arrived, displaying a bewildering range of deformities and injuries, the badges of their office. I dispensed some money, much to Ly's disgust, and he shooed them away, though they settled just a couple of metres away from us, and each time I glanced over at them they would smile and rattle their cups, perhaps hoping for a second round of charity.

Equally magically, a corps of young soldiers broke through the jungle that bordered the road and the basilica complex. They were on some kind of military exercise, dressed in fatigues with their faces smeared in camouflage paint. They were all terribly young and terribly hot, their clothes wet through and sweat running down their faces. They displayed none of the discipline for which the Vietnamese army is famous. Upon seeing me they beamed excitedly, and stopped to gather around me and ask questions. Eventually their senior officer, who looked like a schoolboy himself, caught up with them and shouted at them to resume their exercise. They unwillingly fell into line and jogged slowly and heavily up the muddy road in single file, each soldier holding out in front of him what, to my untrained eye, looked like a machine gun. Their presence outside the holy Marian shrine was incongruous in the extreme.

Ly looked wistfully after them.

'Great kids,' he said, 'doing their bit for their country. I wanted to enrol in the army myself.' I was surprised at this. From all that I knew about Ly's past, I had gathered that discipline was not his strong point. 'Oh yes,' he assured, seeing my surprise. 'The army life is the only one that could have made me really happy. But they wouldn't take me—because of my tattoos. The minute I took my shirt off they said, "Can't take you—you look like a ruffian." I was so sad.' Ly sighed. 'I have done so many stupid things in my life. I really want to change now.'

CINNAMON CITY

For me the scent of Hue will always be cinnamon. The incense there is scented with cinnamon. The toothpicks they give you after your meal are made from cinnamon wood, and the exquisite flavour fills your mouth. Children buy slivers of cinnamon bark as after-school treats. In *The Sacred Willow,* Duong Van Mai Elliott's gorgeous memoir of her aristocratic Vietnamese family, she describes a wonderfully picturesque occasion in which her great great uncle, on attaining his doctorate, is awarded by the emperor a gift of cinnamon bark. In antique times, the emperor would carry cinnamon bars in his hands. Ly smoked a brand of cigarettes flavoured with cinnamon, and the smell impregnated his clothes and hair.

In Hue I always wanted to use the beautiful purple rice-paper fans that are sold cheaply throughout Vietnam, the ones with designs of the Goddess of Mercy pressed into them delicately with pins, but I dared not. Monks might get away with them and look old-worldly and quaintly elegant, but sadly a thirty-something Western man wielding a fan takes on an undeniable air of camp.

For me, hot weather and fans go together. I grew up in the tropics in the days before much air-conditioning. Going to old-time dances with my grandmother, I remember the rows of country ladies taking a break from their foxtrots and Prides of Erin, and pulling a dazzlingly glamorous selection of fans from their glomesh handbags: paper fans, silk fans, lace fans, even palm leaf fans woven by relatives in the Torres Strait. The women would chat and laugh, sipping ginger beers, the sweat streaming down their plump faces, and I would be entranced by the action of their fans, sometimes begging them to turn their cool, hand-forced breeze on me, which they did readily.

Fans were old-fashioned even then, of course. My mother's generation made fun of them. 'You get hotter flapping the fan,' they would scoff, but these hippie kids were missing the point. The hand-held fan is an elegant device, a prop more than an instrument of comfort. And the pleasure of the individually focused, self-created breeze was always exhilarating, worth any amount of hardship.

Hue is delightful because it's one of those sleepy cities in which it seems okay not to do much of anything at all. It's like Macau or Siem Reap, a place that has remained alive because of collections of dead buildings people come to see. Tinh Xa, the monastery belonging to the indigenous Buddhist mendicant order out on Le Van Huu street in Hue's old citadel, is beautifully situated on an island in the middle of a lake, and reached by a long cement footbridge. It is almost always closed, mostly because the abbott is a curmudgeonly old rogue who growls at people who come by and does his level best to dissuade anyone from visiting. Hue keeps the old hours, the schedule that all of Vietnam once kept. Between 11.30 am and 2 pm shops, banks and offices close. Restaurants keep their doors open, but waiters and cooks are normally sound asleep on the cool tiled floors and have to be roused if you are after a late lunch.

'I want to take you to Quang Tri,' Ly said. 'It is my home. It is the poorest province in Vietnam!' He seemed proud of this fact. Since returning home, Ly had had a hard time convincing his friends of the glamour of his previous life in Saigon. Vietnam is full of country-town boys who leave for Saigon, and most only ever return intermittently, coming home every year or two for Tet. But Ly had done the unthinkable, coming home for good with no money, no job and no wife to boast of. The friends who had elected to stay home in the village with their families were largely uninterested in his Saigon stories, and I can imagine he must have been insufferable with his boasts and exaggerations.

'They don't believe I have a foreign friend,' he said. 'When I told them I had to come to Hue to meet up with a foreigner they laughed and accused me of lying. You have to come. I can't wait to see their faces when I walk through town with you.' Since his return home Ly had taken a lowly job as a builder's labourer, and it was something about which he was quite ashamed. This accounted for the darkening of his skin and the changes to his body, which had become noticeably more muscular since his Saigon days. His hands, too, were callused and covered in cuts and bruises, and these took attention away from the scars and pits on his knuckles where he'd once tried to remove his tattoos in a drunken frenzy of self-hatred.

To get to his village we had to take a boat down the river from Dong Ha, the regional capital of Quang Tri province. Because of Quang Tri's reputation for poverty I had expected a horrible place, but instead I discovered a beautiful little city, clean and bustling and filled with friendly people who spoke Vietnamese with such an impenetrable regional dialect that they might well have been speaking Laotian, which I sometimes thought they were. Quang Tri shares a border with Laos, and if you keep driving along Dong Ha's main street you will, after a couple of hours, find yourself in that country. Many people seemed to earn a living doing some kind of smuggling into or out of Laos—I thought it prudent not to probe too much. Later I asked other Vietnamese about the Quang Tri accent and they informed me that it is considered Vietnam's most hideous and unfathomable. Fortunately Ly used his carefully acquired Saigon dialect when communicating with me, and thus acted as my interpreter.

The little wooden boat took us about an hour down the wide river, and we pulled up at a cement dock which led directly into a village market. The stallholders shrieked and cheered when they saw us. Soon we came to the end of the market, an uncovered area where the less established merchants kept makeshift stalls selling a variety of sorry-looking merchandise, constantly exposed to the elements.

A sad-faced but very beautiful woman who didn't look to be any more than forty sat at the most dire of the stalls, a display of banana fritters, clumps of wilting basil and a pile of dry-looking bitter melons. It seemed as though she hadn't seen us, though the people all around her were laughing and joking with us, making impolite comments to Ly and occasionally pulling at the hair on my arms. Ly walked straight up to the woman and, turning to me, said, 'This is my mother.' Unsmilingly, she glanced at me and then looked deliberately in the other direction. Ly had filled me in on the sad details of their lives. She had been the mistress of a married man, sent home to her village pregnant, and then largely forgotten by her lover. Ly was the product of her shame, and they had lived in a shack on the outskirts of the village, outcasts in desperate poverty.

We walked up into the village along red dirt lanes. It seemed almost an idyllic site, hugging the bend of the river, at each turn a splendid view of the water. 'This is really beautiful,' I said.

Ly looked embarrassed. 'Very poor,' he said.

We walked through the village, with people calling out Ly's name from inside their houses and children rushing up to look at us. We went through the gate of the biggest house I'd seen in the village. Like many homes in Hue and its surrounds, it boasted a splendid 'spirit house' in its front yard painted a turquoise green. The people of central Vietnam are great believers in spirits and construct the houses to them as an apology for disturbing their territory.

'This is my aunt's house,' explained Ly. 'She is the richest woman in town.' Taking our shoes off before entering was, in this case, a necessity, as they were thick with red mud; I was reminded of the ancient reasons behind the Vietnamese habit of removing the shoes before going indoors. Visitors to Vietnam are often unaware that the shoeless convention is every bit as important here as it is in such countries as Japan. An invaluable investment before travelling to Vietnam is a good pair of walking shoes that can be easily slipped on and off; I have seen too many awkward Westerners struggling in doorways lacing up their expensive desert boots or Nikes, while the Vietnamese around them serenely kick off their far less cumbersome footwear.

His wonderfully plump aunt greeted us and, within minutes, rustled up a truly delicious banquet centred on slices of cold pork wrapped in rice paper and dipped into a fiery hot sauce. She threw woven mats down on the floor for us to eat on, and several elderly men from the village materialised to share the impromptu meal. I was constantly amazed by the capacity of Vietnamese people to put together meals for large groups with really very little preparation.

As we ate, a row of village aunts sat on the big wooden bed behind us and asked questions about me. Ly assumed the role of expert, and with a fair amount of exaggeration and poetic licence he filled everyone in on my great genius, my importance and achievements. 'He's a scholar,' he boasted, 'and a writer. A good Catholic, too.' There was an appreciative murmur at this. People with firm religious beliefs are always respected in Vietnam, even if the religion is not a shared one.

Prompted by my appalling efforts at Vietnamese, one of the aunts remarked, 'He must be able to speak a lot of languages.'

'Oh, many,' assured Ly. 'Viet, English, Chinese, French, Thai, Khmer . . .' Then I glared at him. His assessment of my skills had now entered the realm of fantasy, and I was terrified that some old man might be called in to speak to me in French—always a possibility in Vietnam. Once in Saigon, a novice had come to my house from the monastery up the road, telling me I was needed. Two foreign men were at the temple asking questions, and no-one could understand them. When I arrived, two young backpackers were sitting in the temple courtyard smoking cigarettes, surrounded by worried-looking monks. 'Hi!' I said, cheerily, but they just glared at me. I tried again, 'The monks have asked me to talk to you—was there something special you wanted to see? They said you were asking questions.'

Slowly taking the cigarette from his mouth, one of the young men said, in a thick French accent, 'We don't speak English.' The monks sighed in relief—they'd heard the word 'English' and were confident that things would soon be resolved.

'Oh, I'm so sorry,' I said, turning to tell the monks that communication was impossible. They in their turn refused to believe that three foreigners couldn't speak to one another. The abbott came down and was genuinely perplexed by this language gap. 'How very strange,' he said, 'foreigners not being able to talk. Are you sure?'

So I decided to publicly disagree with Ly, something I never liked to do in Vietnam where such disagreement is considered the height of rudeness. 'Actually,' I corrected, 'I don't speak all those languages. And I'm not Catholic.'

There was a brief, embarrassed silence until one of the old aunts reached down and patted me on the shoulder. 'Don't be so modest,' she said, 'and tell me—are you married?'

PERFUME RIVER

The night before I was to leave Hue, Ly and I walked once more down by the river, sampling the little cafés that stay open all night along the bank. I say cafés, but they were just little collections of plastic tables and chairs serviced by elderly couples who manned stalls further up the embankment. From our swaying, sinking chairs we watched the boat families prepare their evening meals and bathe in the river, as the boatmen of Hue must have done for centuries. One boatman was the proud father of what seemed like a dozen children, all of them slipping in and out of the water, the oldest doing their laundry as they bathed. This was all happening in the middle of downtown Hue, watched by hundreds of passing people. Ly was contemptuous of the boat families. 'They are constantly having children,' he grumbled. 'The poorer they are, the more children they have. One every year. They are a disgrace.'

He was determined to get drunk, mostly because he liked to but also because this was officially a sad occasion, and Vietnamese like to formally celebrate 'occasions', be they happy or sad. Each time we walked a few metres down to the next little impromptu café, Ly would order a beer and then deliver a soliloquy about how sorrowful he was, and how much he hoped my next visit might be soon. Hue lends itself to melancholy, and at many of the surrounding tables there were other groups of men looking sorrowful and drinking their coffees in an austere silence. I was sticking to iced coffee, which in Hue consisted of the traditional filtered coffee mixed with condensed milk and poured over a big slab of ice. The more usual coffee served over crushed ice was known in Hue as *café Saigon* and Ly had forbidden me to order it, it being viewed as an unnecessarily girlish refreshment. In fact, the taking of milk at all with one's coffee was viewed as flirting dangerously with effeminacy, but seeing as I was a foreigner exceptions could be made.

At one café the table next to us was made up entirely of women, an unusual sight in Vietnam where cafés are still viewed as vaguely disreputable and very much the domain of men. Women do visit them, but normally in the name of romance, and they spend their time there snuggled up with boyfriends in darkened corner seats. Even more unusual, these women were loudly, riotously drunk. They stood and proposed toasts and urged each other to swallow their drinks in one gulp. Ly was fascinated by the group.

'Look at those women,' he whispered. 'They are acting exactly like men.' And, indeed, some of them were. The leader of the group was fat and very butch, dressed in jeans and a man's shirt, and every time she sat down from proposing a toast she drew into an embrace a middle-aged lady who sat by her. I realised that, deep in the night, we had unwittingly stumbled upon a drunken, secret lesbian party.

After some time the leader of the party, whose birthday it apparently was, stumbled over to us clutching a bottle of rice spirits and two glasses. 'Boys!' she slurred. 'I insist you join me in a drink—it's my birthday, and it is most auspicious that I should enjoy a drink with a fine, fat, foreign man.' Ly was only too happy to comply, and as I threw back the alcohol it burnt my throat and left behind an odd, slightly rotten taste. I had been drunk on rice spirits before, and knew that its mysterious ingredients could leave you with a very bad hangover.

Ly grabbed the bottle and poured a shot for everyone. 'Sisters,' he said, 'I too have a toast. My friend here leaves in the morning, and I am desolate with sorrow. I want us to drink to my sadness.'

There was a whoop of approval and, hoisting her cup, the birthday girl shouted hoarsely, 'Sadness, now that's something we women know about. Sadness and loneliness. Let's drink to that. To loneliness!' She threw back her portion of spirit. The rest of us held up our glasses, each barely able to make out the other's face in the night's gloom, each lost in our own thoughts as a cool breeze blew up from the river.

'To loneliness!' we echoed in the otherwise silent Hue night.

GENTLE MOTHER

Kwan Yin, the Buddhist bodhisattva of compassion known to the Vietnamese as Quan Am, is easily the most commonly encountered figure of popular devotion in Vietnam. She has also been a potent spiritual symbol for me throughout my life's journey. The first time I ever travelled to Vietnam I was taken by the porcelain statues of the Goddess that were to be found everywhere—on shrines scattered throughout temple precincts, but also in people's homes and, occasionally, on roadsides.

In Vietnam she is often referred to as Me Hien, the Gentle Mother. This title seems to capture perfectly the quality that appeals so much to people. She is the great mother, filled with a boundless love that is free of judgement and concerned only with mercy. Kwan Yin is the great Divine Feminine that I had never encountered till I came to Vietnam, and ever since has seemed to follow me all over the world. This overtly feminine aspect does not seem to stop men from being devoted to her, and from respecting the qualities she represents.

The first time I visited the Quan Am pagoda, in Ho Chi Minh City's Phu Nhuan district, there was a large gathering of monks for a religious festival dedicated to Kwan Yin and the teaching of the twenty-fifth Chapter of the Lotus Sutra, the text in which her special qualities are enumerated. It was a rainy October morning, and the temple was filled to bursting point. Monks stood crowded even on the footpath, their ceremonial robes reflecting the various shades of orange and gold dictated merely by personal preference and not, as foreigners might think, by sectarian requirements.

I was greeted at the gates by Brother Chuc, who lived in a tiny space right up in the mezzanine of the temple, secretly overlooking the prayer hall, in the merest cell concealed behind the vast statue of the Buddha. It was as though he were housed within the shrine itself, and at any time of the day or night he could glance through the ornate grilles that served as his windows and see what was going on inside the temple. Suspended in the air directly behind the Buddha's head, it was a security guard's box, I suppose, and to reach it we had to scale a ladder and drop down through a hole into the obscure little box Brother Chuc was proud to call 'home'. When I visited with him there, we were constantly lit by the changing colours of the Buddha's vast neon halo just outside his window. Chuc was small-boned and girlish, and later, when we became firm friends, he would drive me around the city on the back of his motorcycle. Such trips were sometimes touch and go, he being entirely incapable of handling my weight.

The temple was also extraordinary because it had been the final residence of Thich Quang Duc, the monk who became world famous by his act of self-immolation at the height of the Vietnam War. In Vietnam he is revered as a bodhisattva, and the temple contains a macabre little museum containing the things that he left behind in his room. The museum is almost never open, though Brother Chuc was in possession of a key and would often open it for me to look through. At the very top of the temple the monks were building a pagoda to contain the relics of the saint—a blackened little heart that had miraculously survived the flames.

Outside the museum stood a large statue of Kwan Yin built atop a massive concrete grotto. The Vietnamese are great lovers of statuary, the bigger and more gaudy the better. People often have idealised concepts of Buddhist temples as places of zen-like calm and simplicity, their interiors exhibiting an Ikea-inspired aesthetic of the utmost minimalism. Nothing could be further from the truth. Temples tend to be jam-packed full of statues, altars spilling over with images of the Buddhas and bodhisattvas, most of them entirely undistinguished by artistic merit or antique provenance. Religious transcendence tends to take place in front of plaster statues of the Goddess of Mercy painted in vivid colours. As an erstwhile fan of maximilism I am always inspired by the devotional mess of most Buddhist temples, and delight in the chipped, peeling and down-at-heel images that are prayed to by the faithful.

Some days I would take my lunch at the Kwan Yin temple,

separated from the monks by my lay status and left to eat alone in a little courtyard decorated with bonsai and hanging ferns and a small statue of the Goddess of Mercy herself. While the monks ate their long, ceremonial meal in the refectory I would sit at my own little table, glorying in the heavenly sound of the monks' voices in chant. Then, when it came time to eat, a smiling but silent young novice would come out to serve me, placing on the table a series of exquisite vegetarian dishes prepared in the traditional style of Hue, where the best vegetarian food is said to come from and where monasteries compete to provide the best examples of that region's delicacies. Meals were taken silently and meditatively, and at the end the monks would clean their bowls and eating utensils in tea at the table and then begin chanting again. One of the novices would come out and make the offering of rice to the hungry ghosts, his long topknot, the sign of his junior status, tumbling almost to his waist. Then the monks would stand and file back into the prayer hall, where they would slowly march around its perimeter chanting the name of Amitabha Buddha.

At the end of such an elaborately beautiful meal I would sneak out a side door and tumble into a taxi in the hot midday sun. Resting for an hour or two on the cool floor of my bedroom, I would fantasise about staying permanently in the monastery, wearing my own grey pyjamas and hiding myself away from the world. In the delirium of the afternoon heat, I imagined I could stay in such a place forever.

MR BUDDHA

In most temples in Vietnam, there is a bell in the main hall. Some bells have pieces of paper pasted to them, each one containing a prayer. And in the afternoons old monks strike the bells softly and regularly, all the while whispering the Buddha's name over and over again. Among the more cultivated, going to listen to the bell is considered a legitimate and restful way to spend the afternoon. Though it may seem wasteful, it really is something you need to do when you visit Vietnam. It is an exquisite example of the delicate Vietnamese aesthetic, and exactly the sort of thing tourists rarely bother to do.

I say 'strike the bell', but within a temple this construction is never used. In Buddhism no form of violence is condoned, not even toward a bell. So instead monks use the phrase 'inviting the bell to sound'. And each time the bell is 'invited', the message of

169

these humble, pasted prayers is sent up into the celestial realms, hopefully to catch the ear of a helpful Buddha or bodhisattva.

If I visited Sister Truth's nunnery after the lunch and siesta period, around three in the afternoon, a fragile old nun would always be in attendance in the prayer hall, her eyes closed and lips silently reciting a scripture she was attempting to memorise. She would invite the bell, and her visage fascinated me. She had obviously once been a very beautiful woman, and the remnants of her beauty were still there—the perfectly shaped lips, the high cheekbones and the elegant jawline. Her bald head only threw those features into greater relief. But what fascinated me more was the fact that, at some point in her life, she had had her eyebrows tattooed, a common cosmetic procedure in Vietnam and throughout Asia. She had obviously never imagined that she would spend her twilight years as a Buddhist nun, and this little relic of youthful vanity served as its own sort of moral lesson. I always wanted to know about her and her past, but I never dared ask Sister Truth—enquiring about the old lives of nuns is bad form.

Sister Truth's nunnery is in the far-flung outskirts of Binh Chanh, a semi-rural district officially a part of Ho Chi Minh City though in reality no more than a series of sleepy, ramshackle little villages. It takes about forty minutes to reach it on the back of a motorcycle, driving through rice paddies and past dozy buffalo trying to avoid the sun. The houses of the district are situated far apart from one another, each with a high gate, many of them featuring large ceramic Alsatians at the top of the gate posts, a modern adaptation, I suppose, of the more traditional Chinese temple dogs that adorn pagoda gates. The women of Binh Chanh stroll the dusty streets in the vibrant polyester pyjamas of the Vietnamese housewife, gossiping and clutching babies and taking lunch to the men in the fields. It seems an improbable idyll so close to the centre of Saigon.

The only way I knew to get there was to have Kien drive me to the Buddhist University in the north-western suburbs of the city. Once there I would enquire of the sleepy crew of *xe om* drivers and sellers of secondhand mobile phones that frequent the entrance whether Mr Bao was around. He normally wasn't. It was essential that I found Mr Bao, because he was the only one who knew the way to Sister Truth's temple. Someone was invariably despatched to hunt him down and, fifteen or twenty minutes later, the good man himself usually turned up, driving very slowly on his ancient Honda. Mr Bao is exceedingly affable, his face burnt by the sun but always smiling. He often smells as though he's had a liquid lunch. It's hard to place his age, but he must at the least be in his late sixties, one of the old school of motorcycle taxi drivers forced into the trade because, during the war, they had the misfortune to fight on the wrong side and so became pariah people in the Socialist Republic.

Sister Truth was given this distant farm some years ago by a devotee, and she is slowly building a temple complex on the small parcel of land. There is a humble prayer hall and a dormitory for the other nuns who live there, mostly very young orphans or very old widows, all of whom must be cared for by Sister Truth. It is a hard life, but one for which she says she was born.

Sister's main problem is orphans. Hers is a small temple and a small community with very limited space and resources.

But, being in a poor area, orphans and unwanted children are plentiful, and every month she finds a baby dumped on her doorstep, or a desperate mother appears at her quarters begging her to take her children. Almost the entire community of nuns in Binh Chanh is made up of orphan girls who have decided to embrace the religious life (and there is no compulsion to take the robe). The littlest nun is only five, and is adored by sisters and disciples alike. She is very fat and very forward, with two topknots poking from her forehead, the rest of her head shaved.

In spite of herself—for she likes to cultivate something of a hard-hearted exterior—Sister Truth dotes on the child, and spoils her terribly. She had been left by her mother at the temple some years ago, and no-one had ever been back to see or claim her since.

'When she first asked me who her mother was, I told her it was me,' said Sister Truth. 'Lately she has been going to infant school, and after mixing with the other children there she came home one day and asked me who her father was. I told her it was the Buddha. I told her I loved the Buddha so much that he gave me a special child, and that was her.' She called the little novice over and, stroking her topknots, she absently asked her, 'Who is your mother, child?'

'The abbess!' cried the little girl, throwing her arms around the sister.

'And your father?'

'Mr Buddha!' she cried, pointing towards the prayer hall.

'I don't know if I've done the right thing,' said Sister Truth, switching to English so the child could not understand. Her eyes filled with tears. 'I think she knows the truth, but she is so small, I cannot tell her. What would you do?' I dodged the question, having no idea what I might do or say in such a situation.

More recently a young boy had been left at the nunnery by his mother. Eight or nine years old, he was abandoned because his widowed mother had found a new husband, and the man treated the boy cruelly. Because the boy had a slight disability, the new husband despised him and beat him regularly when he couldn't perform the chores he was assigned. 'She said I must take him,' said Sister Truth, 'or else the husband would beat him to death. What kind of country are we living in? After centuries of the Buddha's teachings, people are still at the level where they would beat a poor, disabled boy? Sometimes I despair of my own nation.'

Sister had declared the boy too old to be residing in a nunnery, and advised the mother to take him to a nearby monastery. But the younger nuns intervened, saying, 'Oh, Sister, we must take him in. Can't you see that the monks would never be able to care for him properly? Only we can give him the love he needs right now.' And so, for now at least, the dear boy is living happily at the little nunnery in the middle of nowhere. Of course, as he approaches puberty he will definitely have to leave—the rules require it. But for now he has found a brief place of refuge in Sister Truth's crowded community.

BEGRUDGING COMPASSION

Reciting the name of Kwan Yin is an accepted religious practice, and one that is quite common among laypeople. In times of stress or worry, you take a long rosary of 108 beads in your right hand, and whisper to yourself as you finger a bead: *Nam Mo Dai Tu Dai Bi Quan The Am Bo Tat Ma Ha Tat* (Homage to the Great Compassionate Kwan Yin Bodhisattva). Such recitation calms the mind and reminds the reciter to emulate those qualities of compassionate awareness and undiscriminating love, the qualities of the Goddess that render her unique and praiseworthy.

The *chuoi*, or Buddhist prayer beads, is a common gift and frequently worn as a special charm in Vietnam. Brother Nguyen, the handsome, pale-skinned monk from Hanoi who studies at the Buddhist University in Saigon, gave me many *chuoi*, one almost every time I visited him. We would sit up in the monks' garden of his suburban temple hidden down a bewildering series of back streets and alleys in an inner suburb.

As soon as we would make a turn down one or two alleys, our improbable appearance balanced on his motorcycle would be too much for the local schoolboys, who would follow us down the alleys laughing and making rude comments. Straining as fast as they could on ancient pushbikes, these laughing boys in their white shirts and red kerchiefs would pursue us all the way into the temple complex, until they were shooed away by the fearsome monastery caretaker.

The monks' garden was on a secluded terrace three storeys up, looking out over a large statue of Kwan Yin flanked by her two attendants. Thay Nguyen would tell me miraculous stories of the Gentle Mother, and explain to me the overwhelming importance of *Metta*—the presence and force of loving-kindness. There is a Buddhist blessing which says: *May all beings, wherever they are, be at peace. May they be free from suffering in mind and body.* For Brother Nguyen this chant encompassed the spirit and meaning of Buddhism, and to recite it unleashed the energy that suffuses the monasteries and nunneries of Vietnam—a simple but absolute regard for every living being. Not mawkish—in fact, always sensible. But palpably there.

'If you find time,' he urged, 'just chant her name. For the name contains the meaning, and the force of her mercy. It doesn't matter if you chant it once or twice or a thousand times. Just keep it with you all day long. If you remember her name, then she is with you.'

Kwan Yin's presence infuses the Vietnamese spiritual landscape, and if at all possible I think visitors should find a shrine and offer some flowers and incense to her while they are there. This could be both an act of respect and of acknowledgement. There is so much to pray for in Vietnam, so whispering a special prayer to the Gentle Mother at a shrine is certain to carry a greater impact than more humble efforts in a hotel room.

Though I tried to recite Kwan Yin's name, I found myself slipping constantly back into anger, impatience and exasperation. I had become so weary of people asking me for money. It was relentless; friends, strangers or acquaintances, it seemed inevitable that, at some point in the relationship, it was deemed okay to ask me for money. In my mind I understood—they were poor, I was rich, and this was a communal culture in which it was perfectly acceptable for the poor to ask the rich for money.

But in my heart I was worn out. I felt used and abused. I thought it was just me, my precious capitalist Western ways. But when I asked Kien, he too confessed that when people he knew and liked asked him for money, he felt incredibly disheartened. 'It's as though they were never really your friend,' he said, 'that they were only ever being nice to you in order to find the right time to beg. This is one of the reasons I hate Vietnam.'

Recognising people's real needs is, of course, one of the marks of the bodhisattva, and even more important is supplying those needs. But by my third month in Vietnam I felt more like a selfish monster than a beneficent bodhisattva. It seemed to me that the longer I was there and the better I got to know people, the more likely it was that they would ask me for money. My anger at this, my depression at feeling used, only increased my melancholy. I was acting like a first-world bore.

I was rich compared to the people asking for money, and I frequently lectured people back home on these imbalances. And yet I felt angry at those who so brazenly tried to leech off me. They were *lazy*, I thought, and not deserving of my hard-earned cash. But when I reflected on my own life I realised that they were no lazier than I was, in fact probably a good deal less. What I wanted was for people to be nobler than I myself would be in the same situation. And I had to admit that for all my moral bluster, I expected something from them—diversion, amusement, friendship, loyalty and interesting stories. Who's to say that they weren't worthy of reimbursement for providing me with those things?

The Elder Nun Tri Hai used to say that by simply reciting Kwan Yin's most sacred mantra, *Om Mani Padme Hum*, we can instantly bring our mind and body under her spiritual control. No matter how filthy the path before us might seem we are all capable of walking on lotuses, because evil is merely an illusion. Kwan Yin's presence is in fact omniscient, and so we are never unaccompanied by the transformative power of compassion.

Some days, however, I found it hard to embody compassion. It was easier to get mad, or harbour a grudge. I did a lot of things I hope the Goddess never saw. Or if she did, perhaps she will extend her famous forgiveness toward even me.

GAS MASKS
AND GOGGLES

If you drive down Nguyen Trai into Saigon's District 5 on any night you will find yourself caught in a gridlock of traffic. This is old Cholon, the heart of the massive Chinatown that once served as a city within a city, home to generations of Chinese who rarely left its borders and who grew up, lived and died here never learning to speak Vietnamese. Anything can be found or bought in Cholon, and each street seems to specialise in its own unique type of merchandise, every shophouse seeming to have conspired to offer the exact same merchandise as the one next to it. One street will have metal shoe and hat stands thrusting out into the oncoming traffic, but turn right and the next street will offer nothing but papier-mache dragons' heads and all the accoutrements of lion dancing.

The old mercantile spirit is alive and well in Cholon,

though the Chinese fled in massive numbers following the Communist victory in 1975. Nguyen Trai is home to shops and street stalls selling cheap but fashionable clothing imported from China, and the throngs of young people, the smell of food being cooked outdoors and the occasional snatches you might hear of Cantonese or Teo Chiew dialect bring alive the sense of what Cholon must once have been like.

If you can hop on the back of a motorcycle taxi at 8 pm and take a leisurely spin down Nguyen Trai, you will be immersed in the real life of the city. The beautiful, youthful residents of this vast metropolis surround you at every side, and whenever something interesting happens traffic grinds to a halt as everybody takes a good look at the passing distraction. Jumping off to enjoy a little bowl of *hu tieu* noodles or a quick glass of freshly squeezed sugar cane juice, nothing is more exhilarating than the energy of Cholon at night and feeling that you are a part of it.

It was in Cholon that the young heroine of Marguerite Duras' novel *The Lover* was kept in a boarded-up shopfront used exclusively for the young Chinese merchant's sexual liaisons. It was in Cholon, too, where the irascible Frenchman Count Gontran de Poncins wrote his wonderful travel classic, *In a Chinese City*, one of my favourite books about Vietnam, though it's not about Vietnam at all. Poncins' thesis was that, at the time he was writing (in the fifties), Cholon was the only place in the world where the Chinese still lived exactly as they had in the China of old, unmolested by Nationalist or Communist forces introducing ideas that had been shaped in the West. One can still catch glimpses of the old Chinese city in the various temples that remain in Cholon, though these, too, are beginning to fall victim to another globalising force—that of Taiwanese Buddhism.

Every time I travel back to Vietnam, the folk religion temples of Cholon, most of them centuries old, become more and more sanitised parodies of themselves. The chaos and superstition of old are being slowly edged out. Floors are being swept and statues are being dusted. Security guards are being employed while shamanesses are shown the door. It's as though people have become ashamed of the old religion and want instead to be able to define themselves as something more solid, to identify with a philosophy that actually has a name and a definable ideology. Cashed-up Buddhist organisations from overseas are happy to contribute to such institutions as long as they attempt to comply with a set of guidelines that invariably cause the temple to identify as Buddhist, glossing over its recent history as an anarchic centre of folk belief and occultism.

The real religion of the Chinese people is something ancient and indescribable, absorbing the spiritual ideas of millennia and offering the individual a riotous assortment of private devotional practices that hinge largely on the veneration of the ancestors, the appeasement of local spirits and the cultivation of quite specific deities related to one's clan, region or occupation. In the Chinese spiritual world Buddhism is a recent arrival, and in general most Chinese temples, particularly those constructed by communities abroad, were never intended to be Buddhist houses of worship. The special Chinese genius saw, of course, the absorption of the entire Buddhist pantheon into the world of popular worship, but in most people's eyes it was rarely the main focus and certainly never the only religion represented in their temples.

The Kwan Yin temple in Cholon, though ostensibly dedicated to the Buddhist goddess, is in fact still a repository for dozens of different deities and spirits. So many, in fact, that staff at the shrine have a hard time identifying some of them. It is situated down the romantically named Lao Tzu street, within walking distance of several other temples as well as a porno theatre, a gay sauna and several hundred brothels. You've got to love Cholon.

I visited the Kwan Yin temple as often as I could, primarily because of the special connection I felt to the Bodhisattva herself but also because I befriended the temple assistants and other workers there, and they would hide me away in some quiet corner and feed me buns that had been offered to the statues by the faithful. I wasn't quite sure about the etiquette of eating such sacred food, but I figured that they were the experts and wouldn't have offered it if it wasn't perfectly acceptable.

People came to the temple for all kinds of reasons: because they were praying for something special in their lives, because it was a date of some particular significance to them, and also to memorialise their ancestors. For this purpose, enormous red coils of incense were purchased at the temple office to be suspended from the ceiling in the main hall. These coils burn for days or weeks at a time, a little red rice-paper tag dangling down from the middle of them bearing the name of the family or individual in Chinese characters. On festival days the incense is so plentiful that staff need to wear gas masks and goggles in order to continue their duties.

I was always faintly self-conscious when making my way around the shrines with my bundle of smoking incense. Sometimes I drew stares and sometimes people would follow me around, figuring maybe that wherever I paused to offer incense would be a lucky spot. People in Vietnam are often looking for a luck angle, and an obviously prosperous foreigner is bound to be a good lead. If I wore a shirt with numbers on it, for example, the people in my neighbourhood would buy a lottery ticket containing those same numbers. Or if I came home in a taxi someone would dash out and jot down the number plate, not for reasons of guaranteeing my safety (which, in my vanity, I initially thought), but in order to use the number as another lottery guide. I became used to being everyone's personal augury.

Sometimes, too, I felt a fraud because at half of the shrines I didn't know who or what was being venerated. But after some time I realised that most of the other worshippers were equally, if not more, clueless, and that even some of the staff were hazy about the more obscure statues sitting blackened in forgotten corner shrines. I made a special cult of those, figuring that they were somewhat neglected and in need of an energetic boost. Some among my friends would be horrified by my wilful idolatry, but in my turn I would be appalled at their overly simplistic understanding of ritual. If I knew the qualities of the figure venerated, I could offer incense and reflect on those qualities and how best I could cultivate them. If the deity was a mystery to me, the act of offering became a simple prayer, an opportunity to recall loved ones and people I knew in difficult situations and to pray for their happiness.

THE HERMIT
ON THE HILL

A group of young monks and nuns from the Buddhist University had organised an impromptu day trip to the beach, supposedly in my honour, but I suspect more for the benefit of their recreation. Such trips, when undertaken by monastics, always begin at an improbably early hour, and I had been instructed to wait for their bus outside the university at 5.30 am.

Travelling to a beach resort with a bus full of Buddhist monastics is always fraught. What to wear, for a start. It is frankly bad manners to wear short pants in the presence of a monk or nun, so that pretty much cuts out most standard beach wear. Later, when it came time for a swim, I embarrassed myself by emerging from the change sheds shirtless. All the monks had on modest cotton t-shirts, which they wore into the surf. Of course, everyone's eyes were on my enormous, hairy form.

Such trips to the beach are impossible to avoid if you spend any time in Vietnam. Each and every resident of Ho Chi Minh City seems to dream of taking a day off to enjoy the long white beaches of Vung Tau, and perhaps climb up the mountain that overlooks it and catch the view from the vast statue of Jesus that stands sentinel over the coastline.

I remember once I visited one of the private beaches of Vung Tau with family and, lying back on a deck chair soaking in some rays, half-asleep, I suddenly felt hands running through my chest hair and then pinching my nipple, hard. Thinking it unlikely that a family member would feel the urge to do this, I opened my eyes and sat up to discover that one of the beach's armed security guards had been responsible. Needless to say, it is always distracting to discover oneself being fondled by a heavily armed man in full view of onlookers. The other guards and workers watched in approval as the buff security man turned his attention to my entirely un-lovely back hair and, stroking it reverently, said, softly and simply, '*Dep, dep lam*. Beautiful, so beautiful.'

On the way back from the beach, one of the nuns on the bus insisted we take a detour to meet an old teacher of hers. 'He lives on Mt Yen,' she assured us. 'Very simple to find.'

After about ninety minutes of detours and perilous off-roading, our chartered bus driver simply refused to drive any further and veered into the parking lot of a nearby nunnery and pulled out a newspaper. 'You crazy priests can scale as many mountains as you like,' he said. 'I'm not ruining my van for anyone.' The nun began to remonstrate, but the driver stared fixedly at his newspaper and we were left stranded.

'Well,' said the venerable sister, 'we are only about ten minutes' walk away.'

And so we began to scale Mt Yen, the mystical mountain retreat about an hour outside of Ho Chi Minh City. The Ba Ria Vung Tau district has always been a different administrative zone to the big city, and the local authorities there have, almost since 1975, taken a more lenient view of religious institutions. So while for decades it was almost impossible to build any new religious structure in Ho Chi Minh City, in Ba Ria it was anything goes, and temple after temple, monastery after monastery, was erected. The religious communities were founded on such a scale that the old road from Saigon to Vung Tau became a veritable tour of the Vietnamese spiritual landscape, Theravada temples standing cheek by jowl with Franciscan nunneries.

The most crazy and mystical religious practitioners have always headed to the hills in Vietnam, and the country is littered with sacred mountains that have, probably since the dawn of time, harboured more than their share of lunatics, zealots, petty criminals and religious rebels. Mt Yen has, for a long time, been one of the most famous of these, and the little nun's teacher was just one of these zealots, having set up shop all alone on the very top of the mountain.

The walk was interminable, agonisingly hot and humid, and all of us were already exhausted by a morning's frolic at the beach. I was becoming more sunburnt by the second when a monk on a little scooter loomed in front of us and drew to a polite, sputtering halt. He was a camp little fellow, his face wrinkled, and he was wearing, somewhat improbably, the bright yellow ceremonial robes usually reserved for prayers and official functions. 'Why, I could hear you all from the top of the mountain!' he cried, casting a happy smile over us. 'Are you coming to visit me?'

'Well, Brother,' groaned the nun, 'I hardly think we'd be making such an effort in the sun for any other reason.'

'What fun!' he trilled. 'See you up there!' And he promptly turned his little scooter around and sputtered back up the mountain.

After a further fifteen minutes of hiking we rounded a corner of the pebbly little road and there it was, a truly remarkable collection of caves and rock formations at the very top of a hill, announced by a rickety handpainted sign saying 'Amitabha's Mountain'.

The little old monk was clapping his hands and leaping up and down in an arbour he'd created by the cave. 'Come quickly!' he shouted. 'Oh! To have such illustrious visitors!' We plonked ourselves down at the cement tables arranged inside the arbour, the monks and nuns dividing themselves naturally. The monk ran over to me and threw his hands around my neck. 'Oh, welcome, Brother! What is your name?' I told him and he brushed it aside with a worried smile. My name is almost impossible for Vietnamese to pronounce, and its odd collection of sounds seems as improbable to them as those extraordinarily long and implausible Polish or Czech names seem to an English speaker.

'My name,' he said, 'is Mountain. But you can call me Amitabha!' At this he let out a shriek of girlish giggles, while the other monks just stared at him. He was extremely eccentric, and the fundamental distrust city monastics have for hermits and mountain dwellers was obviously rising to the fore. He had just asked me to call him by one of the Buddha's names, something absolutely beyond the pale, and whether meant in jest or not it was a statement that made the monks distinctly uneasy.

'I am a simple man, you see,' he began to explain. 'I live alone on this mountain. I have been here for twenty years now, and doubt I shall ever go back down. So I no longer have need for a name. You can call me by the mountain's name, or call me by the Buddha's name, for all is one in the Buddha.' Such an unusual theology was still too much for the city monks, and they began to whisper among themselves. I, on the other hand, was rather taken by the old rascal, and asked him to show me about his hermitage.

It really was the most incredible place. Three enormous rocks had fallen together to create a cave and this the monk had transformed into a prayer hall, with a statue of the Buddha at one end and, high up in the rocks at another, a beautiful, simple statue of Kwan Yin. On a cliff he had built a rather perilous veranda commanding a sublime view over almost the entire province. This was where he ate and where guests could sleep. 'There are only mosquitoes,' he said, 'if it is windy.' And at this he broke into another of his insane peals of uncontrolled laughter. His social skills seemed quite undeveloped, and he obviously didn't get out much.

Around the other side, in another natural cave formation, he had constructed his abbott's room, an essential part of traditional Vietnamese temple design. It was here that he slept and meditated and conducted interviews with visitors. He had decorated it beautifully, and there was even a row of bookcases and a jagged stone wall of framed photographs.

We all sat cross-legged on his windy veranda and the younger nuns quickly prepared the most wonderful meal, seemingly out of nothing: a salad made of shredded rice paper and mountain herbs stirred up with soy sauce and blisteringly hot chilli, and big plates of mandarins and sliced dragon fruit. A nun sang a beautiful song to us before we ate, in a voice that I imagined carried down this quiet and mystical little mountain and washed over all the communities below it.

While we were eating one of the monk's telephones went off, and the ring was the chanting of Kwan Yin's 'Great Compassion Mantra', a long tongue-twister of a mantra that was so beautiful it gave me goosebumps. Its application to modern technology delighted me, and no-one blinked as the monk stood and rushed out to chat to the person on the other end. The mantra had somehow neutralised the technological imposition in this quiet place that was without even electricity.

The mountain hermit beamed at us as we sat there; possessed of old-fashioned manners, he had refused to eat with his guests. Instead he ran the rosary through his fingers and kept the conversation rolling. 'There is only one thing you need to remember,' he said to me. 'In the true community of the Buddha there is no master and servant, no teacher and student. Everyone here has been your mother, your father, your friend. Over and over again we have sat together like this, enjoying the mountain air—we just can't remember it any more. But don't imagine there are divisions between us, foreigner and Vietnamese. That is only in this lifetime, and this lifetime is short and precious. So don't call me Master and don't call me Teacher.'

He smiled his toothless smile and leaned forward to heap some more salad onto my plate. Returning to his rosary, he resumed his train of thought. 'Just call me Friend, that is respect enough,' he said, running the black glass beads through his fingers.

'Your old friend on the mountain.'

PASTEL PINK
AND PORCELAIN

Strolling home one day from the Buddhist University, I had planned to stop in at the little scholarly coffee shop on the way, the place I called Café Tien Si (the Doctor of Philosophy's Café) on Thich Quang Duc road. The streets of Ho Chi Minh City make for rather desperate exercise for even the most enthusiastic of pedestrians. Footpaths can vary wildly, and occasionally disappear into deep drains. When they are not serving as motorcycle parking lots they make excellent extensions of shop display space, and so the Saigon flaneur must spend much time walking in the road itself, right in the midst of the traffic, praying wildly that a bus or truck doesn't come speeding up behind you.

But as I was walking along the road Brother Great Belief, driving against the traffic on the one-way street, pulled up alongside me on his motorcycle and said, 'Hop on, Fat

Brother—I'm taking you home.' Foolishly, I climbed aboard, and from that moment I was his prisoner. 'You've got time, haven't you?' he asked. 'Let's go visiting.'

Temples are usually closed between eleven and two. The monks rise early and so a lunchtime siesta is essential, and besides, this schedule is ordained by the Buddha himself—apparently he was partial to an afternoon nap. Brother Great Belief took me to his home, which happened to be Vinh Nghiem temple, Ho Chi Minh City's largest, during the rest time. I wandered about the monks' quarters in the quiet haze of the hot lunchtime recess. Monks could be seen through cell windows snoring or reading. No-one was really interested in my presence. Lunch was over and afternoon work was soon to begin, and the getting of rest or leisure was all that was on their minds. Brother Great Belief had taken the precaution of asking one of his seniors if he could have special leave to entertain a guest during this unusual time, but even the senior monk was uninterested, waving him and his request away. 'Do what you want,' he said, returning to his newspaper.

Underneath Vinh Nghiem's main hall was a series of large rooms used to teach monks, give sermons and feed the community. It was shady and dusty, the rooms crowded with the heavy black wooden furniture so beloved of monastics. In the refectory the dining tables and chairs were particularly beautiful, inlaid with dragons and phoenixes rendered in mother-of-pearl. At the head of the room was a large shrine bearing the image of the revered founder of the temple; Brother Great Belief lit some incense for me and together we bowed to the late monk's memory.

I find it fascinating that the Vietnamese reverence for ancestors is transposed to a monastic setting. Monks memorialise not the ancestors of their genetic family, but the great patriarchs of their monastic lineage. They are capable of naming their religious antecedents back several generations, and each temple contains a shrine to the masters complete with photographs of the abbott's own teachers. The abbott, particularly the ordaining abbott, serves in a very real sense as father of his monastic community, and the monks care for him and revere him as they would their real father.

Brother Great Belief liked to have me around in the *van phong*, the reception office of the temple where he worked several days a week. Seated at the long table, he would supply me with endless glasses of iced water, which necessitated my endless visits to the monastery toilet, inevitably flooded. 'Do you know,' he said, looking a little excited, 'that we have a Westerner living here?' This threw me a little. For many years the government had made it impossible for foreigners to reside at temples and monasteries, and had forbidden their ordination in Vietnam.

'A monk?' I asked, incredulous.

'Yes—do you want to see him?' I wondered if perhaps he was kept in a cage. But yes, I certainly did want to see such a creature. Brother took me down to the row of VIP cells usually kept for senior monks. These were reasonably spacious rooms on the cooler ground floor: private, with wooden shutters and lockable doors. Knocking on the old door, a thin Englishman of early middle age, wearing the brown robes of a Vietnamese monk, opened the door. We both bowed low to him, and he looked embarrassed and slightly annoyed. Great Belief began to address him in English, but his English was such that it was totally incomprehensible. We chatted for a while; the English-man had been ordained in Burma but had recently moved to Vietnam, which I can only imagine must have been an enor-mous Buddhist cultural shock.

He was personable enough to me, but his dismissive atti-tude towards Brother Great Belief I found boorish. The fact was that Great Belief was actually his monastic senior by many years, and so was deserving of respect. In the Buddhist monas-tic tradition, one's age in calendar years counts for nothing. It is the years spent ordained that are important, and so a thirty-year-old who has been a monk since he was twelve far outranks a forty-year-old who took the robe a couple of years ago. But Great Belief was never one to stand on ceremony and remained beautifully courteous, if not outright worshipful, of the exotic Western monk. This lack of humility is something I have fre-quently observed in Western monastics, and seems to me to be the quality and discipline they should concentrate on above and beyond meditation.

When we came back to the *van phong* a woman was patiently waiting, clutching a pastel pink porcelain statue of Kwan Yin. These pink statues seemed to be all the rage, and I had noticed in the Buddhist gift shops rows of expensive pink statues of Sakya-muni, Amitabha and the Medicine Buddha, too. 'Master,' she said, 'may I leave the statue here to be blessed?'

'Certainly,' said Brother, gesturing toward the office altar, which was unusually crowded with statuary, images and other religious objects. When the woman left Brother explained that people bring the objects to the temple to be ritually blessed and rendered ready for proper worship. For three days they are left on the office altar, and the monks pray over them three times a day. Everything important in Buddhism is done in threes, that number representing the three objects of refuge: the Buddha, the Dharma (his teaching) and the Sangha (the Buddhist community, especially of monks and nuns). One always offers three sticks of incense, for example, and bows three times before an altar.

People seemed to bring in everything that might be used on the family altar, not just statues and framed images, but also brass candlesticks and porcelain incense burners. Not only was the altar full to the point of collapse, but several side tables had been drawn up to take the overflow. And even the floor beneath the altar was crowded with spirit houses and wall shrines, there to be blessed before being set up.

I noted one or two statues belonging more properly to the realm of popular religion—the Kitchen God was there, as was the Celestial Empress, both figures well outside the domain of Buddhism. This lapse in orthodoxy seemed not to bother Brother Great Belief. 'Oh, we leave them with their little devotional eccentricities,' he explained. 'Besides, worship is always a good thing. You can't be doing anything wrong with some incense in your hands.'

So often when they visit temples, Western tourists stream in, take a cursory glance around the main hall, then stream back out. But to the Vietnamese the temple is often an extension of their living space. It is a place where people can come to escape the crowded conditions at home. It is always rewarding to spend an entire morning or afternoon strolling around the temple grounds, peeking in at the hidden-away shrines and reception rooms, sitting on the stone benches reading a book or writing in your journal. The monks can be observed following their mysterious timetables, and any number of peculiar rituals might take place spontaneously. The problem with travelling is that so much of what we see is forgotten. To spend a few hours in a sacred space, unhurried and unexpectant, is to create a memory of place that is far more vivid than any photograph.

PATRON SAINT OF HAIRDRESSERS

Chua Ong is a Hindu temple at 66 Ton That Thiep, right in the heart of downtown Saigon, one of the last surviving in the country. It is stuck in an obscure street behind the Fashion TV Café, so no-one really knows about it. It is almost always deserted, completely forgotten among the ritzy boutiques and new foreign banks that otherwise occupy this quarter. The place has a wonderfully sleepy, careworn quality.

The French expended much during the colonial period in attempting to make this part of Saigon an exemplar of imperial possibility. And certainly in downtown Saigon, much of that splendid colonialist dream is still apparent in the wide streets and squares and the carefully restored French colonial buildings. But on the whole such grandeur is lost in the sheer chaos of Saigon traffic, that vast quantity of people pressing ahead and intent on ignoring the order that French architects and city planners obviously hoped to impose.

Operated by a stunningly handsome mixed-race man who also doubles as the priest, Chua Ong (the Mister Temple) is one of those little sacred secrets that make a city so fascinating and could never have been included in any French colonial plan. Kien, the style guru, was convinced that this temple, dedicated to what he saw merely as some mysterious Indian God, must have a special energy for hairdressers. And so, when business was bad, we jumped on his groovy and very fast purple Kawasaki and made our way there to offer coconuts and Indian incense to Ganesh, Mr Elephant as Kien calls him, who is practically the patron saint of hairdressers due in part to our keen patronage.

As we amble about from shrine to shrine, Kien is only vaguely curious about who is being worshipped and what they might represent. For him it is enough that a causal link can be made between visits to Chua Ong and an increase in customers that night at his salon. But he is vaguely mystified as to why there should exist an Indian temple in Saigon where there are few Indian people to be found. All young Vietnamese are very hazy on the pre-1975 history of Ho Chi Minh City, and are largely unaware of what a cosmopolitan place old Saigon was. They have been indoctrinated with a nightmare vision of a gotham of forced prostitution, drug addiction and the presence of foreign oppressors intent on bringing the motherland to its knees. And though, as historian Gabriel Kolko has pointed out, the vast refugee camps that sprang up on the outskirts of the city as a result of the war were horrendous cesspits of poverty and desperation, Old Saigon remained a bizarrely sedate metropolis, elegant and sophisticated. Indian and Chinese traders mixed with the remaining French colonials and the newer class of American military and other workers in a conspiracy to cling to the historical ideal of the Indochinese capital—all of them, of course, fiddling while Rome burnt.

Across town is Chua Ba (the Madame Temple), devoted to the Hindu goddess Mariamman. This place is much more popular, and has tapped into the Vietnamese devotion to the mythic mother. Chua Ba can become distinctly glamorous, particularly in the early evenings when it is visited by young women who work at night, in whatever occupation. They come here to pray for good fortune and good business. The resident Goddess also has a name for providing rich and handsome husbands, as well as guaranteeing male children, so the temple's popularity is almost perpetually guaranteed.

Not so for Chua Ong, alone and unvisited in a part of town that sees little foot traffic. I live in fear that one day it will be demolished, so valuable is the land on which it wastes away. The place is so unused to visitors that whenever Kien and I arrive, someone has to be hunted down to take care of our motorcycle and provide for the devotional rituals. The temple keeper's wife sits on the threshold and keeps an eye on our bike while he tends the ritual fire and brings out to us a little platter containing burning camphor, perfumed water and the various pastes and coloured powders with which we paint *tilaks* on our foreheads.

He would also give us little plastic bags filled with fruit and flowers which had been offered to the deity. Driving home with red and grey dots on our foreheads and ostentatiously clutching garlands of jasmine and honeysuckle, we would re-offer the *prasadam* at the shop shrine to Lord Ganesh, watched intently by the apprentices and whichever customers happened to be there. Kien loved the peculiar ritual of it all, boosting as it did his reputation as sophisticate and lover of the exotic.

I was pleased that remnants of Hinduism still survived. Much of central and southern Vietnam had once been a Hindu kingdom, the Indian-inspired Kingdom of Champa having overseen a largely Hindu population until its defeat by the Vietnamese in 1471. It made me happy knowing that these ancient memories were revived, on occasion, in a humble little hairdressing salon in the suburbs of Ho Chi Minh City.

CAFÉ SOCIETY

To while away one's hours in a café is considered an honourable profession in Vietnam. Go to any café during the day, though particularly the un-air-conditioned ones in the suburbs that cater to the working classes, and you will see men smoking determinedly and working their way very slowly through a black coffee that has been individually filtered over ice. They are never reading, they are never talking. Their job is to look sad, preoccupied or creative. These poses are all acceptable ones for people malingering in cafés.

The traveller, too, is inclined to spend an inordinate amount of time in cafés. Robert Dessaix, that great reinventor of the travel narrative, says in his book *Arabesques* that cafés 'are the quintessence of travel'. Particularly in countries that boast extremes of weather, spending two hours in a café is a reasonably convincing way of telling yourself that you have been out and about, that you haven't been wasting your time in a foreign land, time that you have purchased at such great cost.

And in a crowded country like Vietnam, a café can provide an invaluable semi-private space away from the prying eyes of family. Men come to cafés to work on their laptops, or to conduct personal business very noisily on their mobile phones. Favourite cafés become extensions of a person, and to be invited to one is a great privilege and an indication of trust.

Coffee is an integral part of the Vietnamese diet, serving much the same romantic purpose that wine does in Western culture. Tea, of course, is the more traditional tipple, and is much more commonly consumed by everyone. But coffee retains a risqué, somewhat decadent air. If the man of the house requires a daily cup of coffee to be prepared, this is always surrounded by much pomp. 'Ah, Thuan and his coffee,' the other members of the household will say, rolling their eyes, secretly delighted at the dangerous sophistication of their husband and father. I don't mean to sound sexist in describing this phenomenon, but coffee is still considered a man's indulgence. Women do drink coffee, but it is rarer; in cafés they serve a glass of iced milk which has a tiny bit of espresso poured over it for flavour and colour, and this is what women will tend to opt for. Unlike tea, which is viewed as a health tonic, coffee is seen as an unhealthy indulgence and as such is likely to be eschewed by most women.

Of course, from a business management perspective, the beauty of a coffee shop is its great simplicity. All one really needs to establish a café in Vietnam is a spare front room, or even a shady piece of sidewalk by a temple or wall. Many people across the country have availed themselves of this opportunity, and owner-operator of a café must be among the premier occupations of Vietnam. From the smallest village in the rural north to the crowded boulevards of downtown Saigon, the humble, sparsely appointed café is the single most uniform part of any Vietnamese streetscape.

The presence of coffee in Vietnam, and its absorption into popular culture, is of course a result of the years of French colonialism. Vietnam is surely the only Asian country where coffee and bread, in the shape of crusty baguettes, are both a part of everyday consumption. Cheese is also consumed, normally from the round boxes of *La vache qui rit* and its various local rip-offs. But this is considered an even more cultivated taste, and many Vietnamese remain unable, and totally unwilling, to take cheese. Kien, who was always interested in ways to gain weight—an abiding fascination among young men in Vietnam, many of whom deplore the traditionally slender forms of the Vietnamese male—was fascinated by what I ate when left to my own devices. He soon added cheese, peanut butter and strawberry jam to his culinary repertoire, under my tutelage.

Cafés are often distinguished by the presence of one or more big-screen plasma TVs. Mercifully they almost always have the volume off, leaving the viewer with a thrillingly cryptic parade of images upon which to impose one's own script. *Fashion TV* is a great standby, as is any film involving children, chimpanzees or Jean-Claude Van Damme, who is still oddly popular in Vietnam. Another great favourite is the glitzy variety show produced in America by overseas Vietnamese such as *Paris by Night*, a series of concerts staged by Vietnamese performers based in California. These are real spectaculars, all singing, all dancing entertainments that stretch on for hours and are often staged in the big casinos of Las Vegas. DVDs of the shows are banned in the Socialist Republic of Vietnam though, almost inevitably, they are also one of Vietnam's most popular entertainments, their presence almost ubiquitous. They are well worth purchasing, and can be done so for less than a dollar at most Vietnamese DVD shops. As entertainment goes they are faultless, even taking into account the language barrier. They are glitzy and sexy, as much paeans to American variety-show culture as they are showcases of Vietnamese tradition.

The ruling regime is probably quite right to distrust the emotions kindled by watching *Paris by Night*. The shows are intentionally works of nostalgia, evoking the memories of mythical golden years when Vietnam wasn't a police state and when the common person was contented and happy, frequently in a straw conical hat. Suffice to say that such days never existed, or only existed in as much as people did wear straw conical hats.

I was in a DVD shop on August Revolution street one day when a strapping young man came in requesting the latest *Paris by Night* DVD, the one advertised on the handwritten sign outside. The cheery shop owner handed him one and the well-built fellow left. A few moments later he came back in, this time accompanied by two uniformed police officers—it turned out it was an undercover sting, and the poor owner was in trouble for selling and promoting illegal material.

I was surprised that I wasn't ordered out, as foreigners normally are whenever the police want to do something sensitive. But right in front of me they began going through the stock, pulling out hundreds of DVDs of American-Vietnamese variety shows, and ordering the owner to take down his wicked posters. I imagine the good people of August Revolution street slept well that night knowing they'd been saved, once again, from the nefarious pollution of a bit of Vegas razzle-dazzle. In modern Vietnam, it would seem that singing and dancing is still a dangerous threat to public morals.

FAMILIAR SPIES

In Ho Chi Minh City I happened to live above a café, but it was a café *binh dan*, an 'everyday café' that was popular with poor university students from the provinces and elderly men with time on their hands. It was very cheap, and there was almost always a table available, but it wasn't at all my kind of place. For a start, the staff was entirely made up of people I knew and lived with, so it was in no way relaxing. If anything it was an invitation to be probed and quizzed about recent and upcoming events, in detail. My movements never ceased to fascinate them, and I was often surprised by the amount they seemed to know about what I did each day. There was absolutely no privacy, and my activities were seen as a stimulating subject of discussion and speculation.

I would often come home to be idly asked how my breakfast was that day: 'You had pork noodles, didn't you? And then you went to the post office in Saigon—was it busy?' I can only assume that a series of neighbourhood spies—the people who lived at the top of our street, the local shopkeepers, the motor-cycle taxi drivers I used—came by at various points during the day to report on what they knew. Most areas of Ho Chi Minh City are really little more than enlarged, intensified villages, and village culture seems to continue unabated.

So to escape such scrutiny I would duck down a series of alleys and emerge on Le Van Sy street, one of Ho Chi Minh City's more congested thoroughfares. That was where *my* café was, a humble enough place that still managed to boast an air-conditioner (which was frequently turned off) and, a rare thing indeed in Vietnam, a non-smoking room. Though being a com-mitted non-smoker, I still tended to avoid the non-smoking room as it was often filled with boisterous, bird-like teenage girls whose chattering drove me to distraction. I preferred the fug of the general café and its almost complete quietness, save for the occasional, inordinately loud telephone conversation.

One day, arriving at the café on Le Van Sy early in the morning, I was alarmed to discover the waiters all stripped to the waist, wielding machetes. Tham, a big, buffoonish Mekong Delta boy, was scaling one of the tall coconut trees in the courtyard garden, machete clutched between his teeth pirate-fashion. Thao, the more reserved fisherman from Mui Ne, quietly put his shirt back on when he noticed my arrival and threw away the cigarette that had been dangling rakishly from his lip. Thao's more decorous nature forced him to make such genteel concessions to a good customer, even when the owner (the fearsome Co Tam) had ordered all male staff to go out and tidy up the garden. I was delighted by the frenzy of unusual activity (the waiters were previously more noted for their languor), but within a couple of minutes I was seated at my usual table and being attended by a number of now-clothed staff, albeit with sweat soaking through their white polyester shirts.

I always think that while travelling, even if you are to be in a place for just a few days, it is worth cultivating a 'local': a place that you visit regularly, and where you tip lavishly. Nothing is more satisfying than to be recognised in a foreign land, and to have people glancing from surrounding tables and wondering who exactly you are. To be greeted by name by waiters halfway across the world is one of life's more satisfying experiences.

Ly Van Sy street and I had something of a *histoire*, and a moderately unhappy one at that. Once, coming home from a rather dazzling night out, I fell badly on Le Van Sy, or should I say into Le Van Sy. Emerging from its justly famous, and truly delicious, late-night *pho* restaurant, I stumbled in the gutter and fell, facedown, right into the busy street. Motorbikes screeched to a stop all around me but, oddly, no-one actually helped me.

Now, I live in a big city so the concept of not being helped isn't exactly a shocking one. But at least at home people have the decency to pretend not to have seen your unfortunate fall. In Vietnam, where people are eternally curious and often on the hunt for a cheap night out, any personal misfortune or public embarrassment is seen as fair game. The Vietnamese are world-champion starers, not to mention sarcastic commenters.

So a small crowd gathered around me, many of them laughing. Most of the staff of the *pho* restaurant came out for a gander, and forever after that would always call out, 'Hey, that foreigner who fell over in the street is here' whenever I came in for noodles. Eventually my friends helped me up, my pride rather more wounded than any part of my body, though I had a nasty gravel rash on my arm that I was terrified would become septic from the filth of the street.

When I told Kien about my mishap, he said, 'Oh yes—you must have offended the spirits of the street. Have you kicked any offering plates over that were left outside? Have you been falling on shrines lately? Perhaps in your last life you were an American GI and killed someone on Le Van Sy and now they have had their revenge? Better you avoid Le Van Sy—no good can come to you on that street.' But there was no way I could avoid the main road that connected my neighbourhood to central Saigon and besides, my favourite café was there.

A year later, I had just got out of a taxi on Le Van Sy and, distracted by the goings-on in a furniture factory on the corner, I once again fell. This time the fall was more violent—maybe because I wasn't drunk. I couldn't say what I tripped on, and it seemed as though I was pushed, though there was no-one around me. One moment I was strolling along the street and the next I was collapsed, again facedown, on the footpath, my arm twisted beneath me and my lungs gasping for air. Again traffic stopped to watch the spectacle, but this time the men from the furniture store came out to assist me, asking how I was, if I needed an ambulance. Fortunately I was a known identity in the neighbourhood, and within moments someone from my house had arrived to look after me and see me home.

That night Kien was beside himself with distress. 'Your karma on Le Van Sy is very heavy. For some reason the ghosts there hate you. You must stay away—worse things might happen. We need to fix this up.' He was still convinced that, in one of my clumsy walks, I had unknowingly kicked and scattered some offerings to the spirits. Such offerings are frequently left out in the street—a small collection of cakes and rice and some incense arranged on a section of banana leaf in order to placate the spirit of the place and any other local genies. 'I don't know why foreigners have to walk everywhere—I told you not to,' he grumbled.

The only way to fix it was for me to make my own offering to the spirit of Le Van Sy. Enlisting the aid of one of the manicurists at Kien's salon, I prepared a fine little selection of rice cakes and chestnut jellies, along with a container of strawberry flavoured milk—a nicely extravagant touch, I thought, which pointed to the offering's provenance. A section of banana leaf was bought for an insanely low amount at the late-night market and, around one in the morning, in order to minimise embarrassment, we made our own hurried little oblation.

It was at the darkened corner of an alleyway where it met the street—no-one seemed to notice except one of the massage boys who circle the neighbourhood at night on their bicycles, shaking rattles to indicate their presence to anyone suffering sore backs or headache. He pedalled over to where we were and watched us intently from beginning to end, slowly edging closer and closer in his curiosity. Strangely, he didn't ask us a single question. He seemed to understand that whatever brought us here, making an offering in the dead of night was of sufficient gravity not to require questions. The act of devotion itself was explanation enough.

TRYSTS AND
DUBIOUS TREATS

The great difficulty I always faced while in Vietnam was avoiding, or getting out of, invitations to tourist parks. The tourist park phenomenon is an odd one, but it accorded completely with the Vietnamese psyche and the Vietnamese love of company. The Vietnamese seem to like to do things in groups. Indeed, solo travel was viewed with horror by most people I met. 'Wouldn't it be so much more fun on a tour?' they asked. 'It must be terribly sad to eat breakfast all on your own.'

Any town worth the name is in possession of at least one tourist park. These establishments are beloved by the locals, who pack them on the weekends, as well as with amorous lovers who take ample advantage of their quietness in the evenings. The Vietnamese have a knack for turning unlikely venues into tourist parks. Orchards seem to be ripe candidates for renovation, but I have also seen monasteries, fish farms, orphanages and even a leprosarium all receive the tourist park treatment.

The irony is that no self-respecting international tourist would ever be seen dead in one of these places, a fact which mystifies the locals. 'Foreigners,' Vietnamese wonder, 'are never happier than when nosing about some dusty old temple or hideous old ruin which should have been knocked down years ago. And all around them are these beautiful venues built specially for tourists! And not even a second glance! Go figure. I know which I'd rather be doing if I had the money or the time.'

The recipe for a tourist park is a simple one, and thoroughly tried and tested. Basically, the government takes over any old muddy lake or industrial waste dump. They fill it with sub-par restaurants, drink and ice-cream concessions, some fun-park rides and a crocodile farm. Bonus points for a cable car, no matter how attenuated or shoddy. Put up a fence and a tollgate charging an extortionate entry fee and *voila*! A tourist park is born. The Vietnamese to a person adore them, and one of the first questions people will ask you soon upon meeting is, 'Have you been to the [insert local name here] Tourist Park yet? It is *very* beautiful. Do you have time tomorrow? I could take you.'

Like many entertainment venues in Vietnam, the tourist parks seem to enjoy a double reputation. By day they are family paradises, filled with hordes of screaming kiddies and shuffling grandparents. By night the pathways and gardens are deliberately darkened and the park becomes a trysting spot, hosting hundreds of couples escaping the supervision of parents and siblings in cramped homes. At night the parks are even popular among gay men, who hope that the romantic licence afforded straight young couples might be extended to them.

Kien had a cousin, a plump restaurateur who, it was whispered, spent all his money on a lean and tattooed martial arts teacher from Binh Dinh who he had installed in a downstairs room. This cousin and his colourful friends spent their weekend evenings at the Dam Sen Tourist Park in District 11 on the outskirts of Ho Chi Minh City, one of the most dire and most popular of the genre. These all-male outings were viewed as further evidence of his debauchery, and among the family 'going to Dam Sen' became the very byword for homoerotic dangerousness.

Another great distraction for this park-frequenting cousin was the collection of 'albums'. These were portfolios of portrait photographs, doctored to within an inch of their lives by freewheeling practitioners of Photoshop in the camera stores of the city. Driving past these studios, the visitor will often see enormous blow-ups of impossibly glamorous newlyweds, or two-metre-high shots of over-accessorised young men draped in unbuttoned shirts exposing rippling chests and torsos. Kien's cousin travelled from one studio to another in a quest for the perfectly doctored shot that would transform him from a squat and squint-eyed man of pronounced plainness into a dazzlingly beautiful male model.

One evening we went to this cousin's restaurant for a meal, but he was nowhere to be seen. 'He's gone to Dam Sen,' said the waitress, who doubled as an aunt. She gave us a knowing look.

'What does he actually do at Dam Sen?' I asked, curious

as to what could possibly be the source of so much prurient speculation.

The aunt/waitress looked puzzled. Obviously she'd only ever been to Dam Sen in the light of day, when its pleasures were innocent and simple. 'Eat apples, I suppose,' she said, reflecting on her own activities at the famous tourist park. 'Durian, too. Sometimes they even have strawberries from Dalat.'

I imagined the plump, gay cousin surrounded by drag queens and rent boys and giggling muscle marys sipping 7 Ups while they sat around a table at Dam Sen heavy with fruit. I was certain it was a metaphor, only I didn't know for what.

SALTED PLUMS

Ho Con Rua, or Turtle Lake, is an absolutely ghastly piece of seventies-era brutalist design that was obviously an attempt to create some sort of culturally significant communal space, but only succeeded in creating a blisteringly hot paved wasteland that serves as a monument to the interesting effects of concrete cancer. It has none of the traditional aesthetics of Vietnamese temple architecture, nor French colonial charm. It is the kind of public construction that would be thoroughly at home in North Korea or some of the newer suburbs of Shenzhen.

Sitting just a block up from Saigon's celebrated Notre Dame Basilica, if you sit around Ho Con Rua long enough you will be harassed and offered almost every commodity and pleasure imaginable. In recent years the lake (which is invariably empty of water, leaving only an exposed, blackened concrete basin) has become surrounded by trendy cafés, and one of my favourites, Café Papas, is just across from it. Late on a rainy afternoon, Café Papas offers the perfect retreat from the city's heat and awful traffic.

The only problem is that often, if customers get a little thin on the ground, the café manager will switch the air-conditioning off in the name of thrift. To compensate for this, waiters will accommodatingly set up a fan blowing at maximum capacity just a few centimetres from my face. The staff seem content to mooch about in the dreadful humidity, their shirts sticking to their backs. 'Oh, it's better for our health this way,' they say bravely, slumping into nearby seats, almost comatose. 'We never had air-conditioning when I was growing up! I'm used to the heat.'

Any potential savings in electricity are almost instantly lost to staff inefficiencies, the waiters slinking outside to take off their shirts and smoke cigarettes, warning potential customers not to go in there, the air-conditioning's off. This stinginess with air-conditioning is seen all over Vietnam, with people convinced that they pay an extortionate rate for their electricity. This may well be true, but I never do have much of a grasp of the real costs of things so the 'outrageous amounts' they quoted to me actually seemed quite reasonable. I would have expected a classy establishment like Papas, with its faux-antique furniture and retro-oriental décor, to be a little less stingy with amenities, but whenever it got down to only one table occupied I sweated with the rest.

During lunchtime, Papas is something of a mecca for tuned-in yuppie office workers who take advantage of the set-price lunches. In the evenings, however, the café is suddenly populated with well-dressed, improbably fit young men who come in groups. Sipping passionfruit smoothies or salted plums immersed in 7 Up, the gay boys are catered for by an in-house DJ who plays a surprisingly satisfying set that is equal parts global gay dance music and Vietnamese pop rock. In what must be the world's most unlikely DJ booth, he sits behind an iron candelabrum at what looks to be a large wooden kitchen table, tablecloth and all, chain-smoking and spinning the platters.

You can almost rely on the fact that the plasma screen will be tuned in to *Fashion TV*, that great passion of urban Vietnamese. Occasionally some witless and obnoxious heterosexual man will request that the channel be changed to an international soccer game, but it never lasts very long. The managing waiter, an acne-scarred but desperately handsome man from the central provinces named Hanh, has no patience for soccer games in his café. Ignoring all complaints, he soon restores the screen to its rightful resting place on *Fashion TV*.

In the quiet afternoons, Hanh would often pull up a seat at my table and tell me his woes. This is an accepted form of social interaction in Vietnam—sharing one's sadness about life's little tragedies. Hanh was learning English, to boot, and saw my frequently lonely presence as an excellent opportunity to sharpen his skills on that front.

Hanh was unlucky in love, his particular fate being a series of lovers who invariably told him lies. Only Hanh pronounced 'tell me lies' in such a peculiar fashion that I really had no idea what his particular gripe was till he wrote the phrase down for me. As an afterthought he wrote beneath it, 'Are you a top or a bottom?' I can only imagine where he picked up this particular question. He asked me to explain it to him and I did my level best, but Hanh seemed particularly concerned in directing that question back to me to actually answer. I refused, explaining it wasn't really the kind of question one asked in polite company. Hanh looked wounded, and told me he'd have no objections to people asking him such a question. So I did, and he answered breezily, 'Oh, both.' But something told me he was lying.

The supermarket in Vietnam is a cultural phenomenon related more to the fun park than to Western ideas of a supermarket. A trip to the supermarket is viewed as a pleasure jaunt, and children will beg to be taken. As well as the supermarket itself, the new breed is really a mini-mall containing electronics shops and restaurants and large bookshops. To get in you normally have to run a gauntlet of poor souls sweating away in enormous foam costumes in the name of marketing. On any day one's way can be impeded variously by an enormous prawn, a ducking and dancing lip balm, and several other characters impossible to identify but large and foamy enough to make negotiating an entrance tricky.

These characters are regularly pummelled and kicked by small children, encouraged by their laughing parents. Older teenagers make a great joke of grabbing them in areas where there is a potential erogenous zone, and this, too, is considered a great lark. I can only imagine the horror of almost asphyxiating in a large foam carrot for eight hours, only to have your bum regularly squeezed and be otherwise violated. Such activity is all part of the supermarket experience, along with attempting to make one's purchases without queuing, watching people withdraw cash from the ATM for twenty or so minutes and standing outside KFC and complaining loudly about how expensive it is.

Outside the supermarket I frequented, the Maximark on Cong Hoa, was a stall which sold a single type of rather intriguing pastry called the Papa Roti Bun. In English it proudly proclaimed that it was 'The World's Best Bun', a claim I was happy not to contest. They were completely round cakes, spongy and fatty at the same time, and rather mysteriously flavoured. Whenever leaving the supermarket I would invariably purchase a packet of the buns, as they were great favourites at home and praised by all as a fine, if exotic and outrageously expensive, snack food.

One day Kien and I were sitting down to a little impromptu brunch of Papa Roti Buns and glasses of sweet cumquat juice we had bought from a stall on the street just outside the salon. Wanting to put my finger on what exactly the buns tasted like, I asked Kien. He chewed thoughtfully and said, 'Cake. I think they are "cake" flavour,' using the English word. I suggested that 'cake' was not a flavour, but described the object we were eating. He took another bite and, after some deliberation, suggested, 'Butter, it must be butter flavoured.'

'Um, well, butter is really an ingredient more than a flavour. This bun has a more distinct taste that I just can't pin down. One that goes well beyond cake and butter.'

Kien continued chewing on his bun, but then he put it

down and turned to me, saying in a disgusted tone, 'Why do foreigners have to know everything? Why do they have to ask such stupid questions? Can't you just accept that it's a Papa Roti? It's a cake, goddamn it. Just eat it and enjoy and stop asking stupid questions. Stop being so difficult.'

I sheepishly took another bite out of my bun, the sounds of our chewing filling up the awkward silence between us. Kien was well into his second one when he suddenly stopped, turned to me and said, 'Vanilla, I think it's vanilla.'

ESCAPE TO
MUI NE

Sometimes I feared I was falling out of love with Vietnam. On some days I would be so furious with the country, with the system, with the people, that I just wanted to go home. It is not an easy place to be for a long period of time, and Ho Chi Minh City is even less accommodating. No matter how you spin it Vietnam is still a very poor country, and the poor are much in evidence. In a big city like Saigon people only just manage to survive, hand to mouth. And, perhaps as a result of the relentless brutality of day-to-day existence, they can be quite disturbingly cruel and dismissive of the suffering of others. Most of the Vietnamese I spoke to were wildly in favour, for example, of the execution of criminals—even quite religious people were convinced of the rightness of this.

I could, whenever I wished, go on a temple crawl, filling

my days with cups of tea and little plates of longan fruit consumed while chatting with monks. But even some of the monks were beginning to grate on me. A whole gang of them from a famous temple in District 5, having decided that I was a handy new loan house, would call me frequently to tell me of some desperate circumstance they had found themselves in that required a hasty injection of my capital.

I began being somewhat reclusive, taking my meals alone in vegetarian restaurants where the bored young waitresses knew me and knew exactly what I wanted to eat. I had been travelling extensively, but the horrendous detail of air travel within Vietnam was one of the contributing causes to my incipient depression. Vietnam's is most definitely not a queuing culture. People push and shove, and if you want to survive for any period of time you quickly learn to join the fray. Those foreigners who stand on ceremony or who continue to line up out of principle must become accustomed to long and fruitless waits, or reliant on rare good Samaritans who will take pity on them and do the thrusting and pushing on their behalf. The unwillingness to queue is one of the greatest sources of disagreement and misunderstanding between foreigners and Vietnamese, and Vietnamese are genuinely mystified when a Westerner gets hot under the collar over the issue. In a crowded country with different criteria for etiquette, pushing wildly is frequently the only way to get from A to B (and then usually back again, with luggage). Since domestic air travel became affordable for locals, trips to regional cities have become insane, with people pushing to check in, pushing to get on the plane, pushing to get off . . . On a flight back to

Saigon from Hue I witnessed a young Thai tourist reduced to tears as she was nearly trampled to death by a tour group of aged widows intent on a good time.

Officialdom provides no respite or solution to the problem of queue-jumping. Airline and post office staff happily serve the first person who thrusts themselves forward, knowing full well that there are dozens behind them who have been waiting patiently. On one occasion I saw a Frenchman be escorted away by security when he erupted in fury at being beaten to the check-in counter for the fifth time, the airline staff blithely accepting whatever tickets were pushed under their noses, completely out of order.

Fortunately my size is a great help in this area. I am simply too big for most people to get past, and if they managed I would merely move forward in a stately but assured fashion, clearing or injuring all in my way. Once I am moving I carry with me a certain grave momentum, and the Vietnamese, firmly grounded in Taoist philosophy, know that it is always wisest to yield to the most solid force.

I only had a couple of weeks left in the country, and I knew I needed to be somewhere nice, somewhere that wasn't Saigon. It also needed to be somewhere I could get to by bus, because if I took one more flight I might quite possibly have turned into a monster. Drowning my sorrows in iced milk tea at the Le Van Sy café, I explained my predicament to Thao, the waiter who was, in truth, a fisherman. 'Ah,' he said, 'Big Brother, I know exactly what you need to do. You need to come with me to my home, to Mui Ne. It is the most beautiful place in all of Vietnam. Do you want to go tomorrow?'

'Can you really get away?' I asked. 'Will they let you take time off, just like that?'

'Oh, don't worry,' he replied, smiling, 'I will just tell the boss that my mother is sick.'

The old sick mother ruse is a popular one in Vietnam. At Kien's salon the employees, whenever they wanted a break, would drag out the sick mother routine and disappear for a few days. They would often come back with a tan, or lots of new clothes. Or love bites. The mothers of Vietnam do it tough, I have no doubt, but if you actually counted the days of work missed or the number of appointments not kept, you would expect every hospital ward in the country would have to be overflowing with ill mothers. But in a country that worships mothers, and the idea of the mother, it is almost impossible to refuse a request made in the name of that ideal.

And so the next day we excitedly boarded the air-conditioned Korean bus heading to Mui Ne on Vietnam's beautiful south-central coast. And all for the sake of Thao's sick mother.

AN INVITATION TO PARTY
IN THE OLD MARKET

I soon discovered that Thao didn't have much in the way of conversation. He was a friendly fellow, always smiling, and having been a waiter since he was a boy, constantly felicitous and mindful of my needs. But once we got to chatting—and on the four and a half hour bus trip there was ample opportunity to chat—I soon discovered the limits of his interests. Basically Thao knew a lot about fish. And what he knew, he was keen to share. He had been born a fisherman. All of his friends and brothers who had remained in Mui Ne were fishermen. So for four and a half hours Thao talked to me about fish.

Fortunately the bus driver slipped on a disc of the latest *Paris by Night* and I feigned fascination, causing Thao to slow down a little in his oratory. By the third hour, the air-conditioned Korean bus to Mui Ne (own seat guaranteed, no extra stops) was a scene of bedlam. I was surrounded on all sides by old women throwing up into plastic bags, while those not vomiting had wrapped their faces and extremities in scarves and jumpers as though we were experiencing a Tibetan winter. 'They are just country ladies,' explained Thao, 'they are not used to the driving, or the air-conditioning, poor things.'

'Poor things,' I echoed as the woman right behind me retched violently, missing her plastic bag but managing to get some through the gap between our seats.

'Such beautiful words,' said the young waiter, snatching my journal from the table. I was in one of those cavernous roadside restaurants constructed simply to serve busloads of people on the way to Mui Ne. Seeing me alone, the young waiting staff zoomed in on me, peppering me with questions and doing their best to decipher my journal. Writing in a journal is always a provocative act in Vietnam, and people are frequently desperate to see what you've written down.

When Thao came back from the toilet the waiters were still passing my journal around. I looked helplessly on. 'They came at me the moment I started writing,' I said.

'You shouldn't write in public around here,' said Thao, testily. 'It's very peculiar behaviour. Of course people will look.'

'But I'm a writer,' I protested, 'you know that. What do you think I would be doing?'

'Vietnamese people don't go about writing in notebooks,'

he insisted. 'It's strange—plain strange. Why don't you use a laptop?'

'I do,' I said, 'but I keep it in my room. I don't like to carry it around.'

Thao looked confused at this. 'Why have a laptop if you're not going to carry it around? If I had a laptop, I would carry it with me everywhere,' he said, somewhat wistfully.

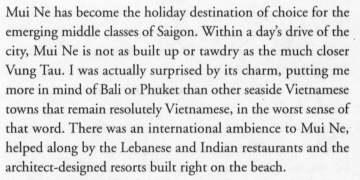

Mui Ne has become the holiday destination of choice for the emerging middle classes of Saigon. Within a day's drive of the city, Mui Ne is not as built up or tawdry as the much closer Vung Tau. I was actually surprised by its charm, putting me more in mind of Bali or Phuket than other seaside Vietnamese towns that remain resolutely Vietnamese, in the worst sense of that word. There was an international ambience to Mui Ne, helped along by the Lebanese and Indian restaurants and the architect-designed resorts built right on the beach.

We drove past all of this luxury and up into a little Viet-namese village that hugged the point and looked down over the long, beautiful beach. 'Welcome to Mui Ne,' said Thao, 'welcome to my home.'

Thao and his family lived in an area of Mui Ne town called Cho Cu, or Old Market. This part of town was defiantly undeveloped. No resorts threatened the paved, hilly streets of Old Market town, no golf courses or high-rise to darken its vistas. Here lived the remnants of what Mui Ne used to be, the fishermen and their families who now did little but provide the restaurants of the Mui Ne resorts with fresh seafood and waved their children off to jobs in Ho Chi Minh City or in the service sector of Mui Ne.

Thao's brothers had remained fishermen and went out each night on the boats, though one moonlighted making shell jewellery and selling it to tourists on the beach during the day. This was a surprisingly dainty occupation for a burly fisherman whose body was covered in the tattoos that acted as good-luck charms to ward off storms and to attract sea creatures.

The houses at Cho Cu were crowded in on one another and the whole village was centred around a large paved common area, the site of the old market, though the market itself was now long gone. It was early evening by the time we arrived, and Thao arranged for a fire to be lit out there and for beer to be delivered. I knew that the beer would be my financial responsibility, but I wasn't prepared for the fact that a spontaneous little village party was about to be organised. As night fell more and more fishermen arrived, pulling out a beer and helping themselves to the fish and prawns that had also materialised (on my tab) and that Thao was busily cooking over the open fire. A man on a bicycle made constant deliveries of boxes of beer and ice.

They were extraordinary creatures, those fishermen. Dressed only in shorts, they were all heavily muscled and their sun-blackened skin was covered all over with the traditional tattoos. It became impossible to guess at their ages, so uniformly powerful were their bodies and so equally sun-ravaged were their faces. They drank and smoke and ate with a passion, and had wonderfully romantic, overtly masculine names like Tiger and Dragon, Strength and Mountain.

One of the fishermen intrigued me. He was tall and as equally muscled and tattooed as the rest, but his hair was long and hung beautifully over his eyes. He was constantly pushing it away in a vaguely coquettish fashion as he fetched beers or cooked seafood over the fire. Though he matched his peers for beer, cigarettes and seafood consumed, there was something that set him apart from the others. He was possessed of a certain poise and gentleness and I wondered what his story was. Catching the direction of my look, Thao laughed and said, 'Don't worry about Vu, he's a homo.'

'What?' I said, not certain that I'd heard correctly the derogatory slang term that encompasses all aberrant sexual behaviours in Vietnam, from gender dysphoria to drunken mutual masturbation.

'You know, he's "gay", man with man,' said Thao, using the English word which was gaining popularity in Vietnam. Vu smiled, knowing he was being talked about.

Another of the fishermen came up to us and joined in the conversation. He fancied himself as something of a polyglot, and attempted to communicate in painful English. 'His whole family, very sad,' he explained, throwing an arm drunkenly around my shoulder. 'His big brother—crazy. And him—homo,' he said.

FISHERMEN'S KARAOKE

Karaoke is an essential part of Vietnam's social culture. It is during karaoke sessions that all manner of relationships are cemented: amorous, business, familial and otherwise. Karaoke bars are ubiquitous, even in quite small towns, and entering a smoky little karaoke room, with its torn faux-leather couches and its microphone featuring superhuman levels of reverb, is a quintessentially Vietnamese experience.

One must always be careful, however, because the karaoke experience covers the whole gamut of social possibilities—from a family sing-song with granny and the kids to a lurid orgy with friends and ladies of the night. Such interactions normally go on in the same venue, which is why a waiter will always discreetly ask on arrival if you want a room with or without an observation window.

I have had to cultivate a karaoke repertoire because

invariably, out of a misguided sense of politeness, most Viet-namese friends insist I be the first to sing when the karaoke machine is fired up. I learned some crowd pleasers through noting which songs were foist upon me after I insisted I would not be singing. The Top Four are: 'Hotel California', the Abba song 'Happy New Year' (even if it is mid June), the Carpenters' 'Yesterday Once More' and an obscure song that is much loved in Vietnam called 'Sad Movies (Make Me Cry)'—the Boney M version.

The whole Vietnamese love affair with Boney M is one of those strange accidents of history that no-one can really explain. During the worst years of state oppression, from 1975 on, Western music was banned, but for some bizarre reason the authorities made an exception for Boney M. What possible reason there could be for this special dispensation I do not know. Perhaps 'Rivers of Babylon' was seen as an exemplary piece of anti-colonialist discourse? Perhaps they thought 'Ra Ra Rasputin' was a pledge of respect to their Soviet allies? Or maybe the stern old Communist cadres just really dug 'Daddy Cool'? Whatever the reason, Boney M survived in Vietnam well past their use-by date. Indeed, in 1994 when I first visited, you could still hear the jaunty tones of their reggae-disco ver-sion of 'Sunny' spilling from almost every shop and restaurant. To this day Boney M is considered in Vietnam to be party music *par excellence*, and a Boney M song is a sure-fire winner at any karaoke get-together.

Sometimes I can be talked into doing Lionel Richie's 'Hello', but that is an extraordinarily difficult song to carry off and hides a surprisingly large range of notes, quickly leading the amateur into perilous waters. To extend my repertoire somewhat I have learned a couple of Vietnamese songs, mostly pop-dance tracks that I remembered from gay clubs in the late nineties. When drunk or hyped up enough to perform one of these, I can normally bring in crowds from surrounding booths. Even staff will drop what they're doing in order to come along and congratulate me as I murder some campy disco tune in their native tongue.

In Mui Ne all the fishermen had insisted we go to karaoke, and so twelve of us jumped on four motorcycles and made our way to their karaoke palace of choice. We sped along in the brisk ocean air, our heads free from the legally required helmets. I was assured that the policemen of Mui Ne are otherwise engaged of an evening, and personal safety is only ever a secondary concern in Vietnam. We drove past the new condominium developments and mini-golf courses that are Mui Ne's great hope.

The karaoke place turned out to be a humble spot in the back of a big garden restaurant. As it was late at night the restaurant was closed, but the karaoke facilities were on offer twenty-four hours. It was a laid-back kind of place, as evidenced by the fact that the waiters took our orders shirtless, one with a towel draped over his shoulder.

Two whole cartons of beer were ordered, and the fishermen industriously set about smoking the maximum number of cigarettes possible. Within seconds the closed-off, hyper-air-conditioned little room was a dark fog. Almost immediately Thao punched a number of songs into the karaoke machine, the first twelve or so being for me to perform. When I demurred he relented somewhat, but insisted I open proceedings with my famously rousing version of 'Hotel California'.

Now, I don't see 'Hotel California' as a particularly festive song, but plenty of people around the world would happily disagree with me. For a start, it goes for about eight minutes, and its dirge-like verses seem to me a bit of a party downer. But at the end of the interminable song, the fishermen all gave me a polite clap and the peculiar performance-point-scorer that spins through at the end of each song came to a whopping ninety-nine per cent, a score which everyone agreed was well deserved.

The fishermen then took turns singing the usual selection of sentimental love songs and heart-wrenching ballads. Occasionally two of them would take to the floor to perform a touching duet, a gruff fellow with a dragon inked onto his massive arm happily singing the feminine role. There seemed not much obligation to actually listen to the performances, only to clap them at the end. One by one the men took turns to come and sit by me as the songs went on, to toast me and tell me long, unintelligible stories.

Thao decided that it was time for me to do my legendary party piece, my guaranteed show-stopping, bring-'em-to-their-knees number. It was a snappy little pop-dance song called 'Loi To Tinh De Thuong' (Words to Express Your Loveliness), a vaguely Khmer-influenced tune that had been a gigantic hit in Vietnam in the late nineties, made popular by a smoky-voiced diva called Phuong Thanh, who at that stage was the most famous person in Vietnam. As well as being upbeat, the chorus has a handy refrain of *ay o, ay ay o*, which seemed almost designed for audience participation.

Once I'd reached that first chorus, the fishermen were up and dancing all around me in that fuggy little room. Indeed, attracted by the noise, the karaoke bar waiters had come to join in the party, shouting their approval as they danced. The fishermen writhed all around me, some clutching beer bottles, some with cigarettes, some clutching each other; all of us deliriously, gloriously drunk.

As we reached the final chorus the *ay o, ay ay o*s reached a crescendo. We sweated and screamed and experienced that corny song with an almost orgasmic intensity. Some of them came to dance by me; Vu weaved around me in a seductive, overtly sexual dance. We were masters of the night, with all the powers of song and dance and lust at our bidding. It was an orgy of musical joy.

At last I understood what karaoke was for.

THE BIG BUDDHA
OF PHAN THIET

As we strolled through the steep little cobbled streets of old Mui Ne town late that night, Thao assured me that the place was thick with ghosts that required constant offerings. This was the particular karma of the people of Mui Ne Old Market—they had to care for ghosts. Certainly I was drunk, but I like to think that it was the ghosts of Cho Cu who caused me to stumble and fall on the unevenly paved streets of the village. My fall was greeted with much hilarity, and I was helped up and brushed off. I seemed to be fine, though the next morning I discovered my side was covered with a massive, ugly bruise and my ankle had twisted badly.

Several of the men suggested we continue with our beer, but I refused. Vu, the tattooed gay fisherman, was fussing over me after my fall and he looked up at me and said, 'Come and stay at my house tonight. I have plenty of room.' There was a hoot of suggestive impropriety from the other men at this, but Thao seemed enthusiastic about the idea.

'Yes!' he shouted, drunkenly. 'He has a nice big house and nobody in it, just the homo and his crazy brother.'

'Yes,' agreed Vu, 'only my crazy brother and me—the rest of my family have gone to America.' So we stumbled down the hill to his house, which turned out to be the biggest and most beautiful of them all in Cho Cu, thanks to a brother who had moved to America.

In the gloriously communal fashion of the Vietnamese village an invitation to me was an invitation to all, and the other fishermen left standing became excited about spending a night at the big house. Vu seemed slightly miffed at their intrusion, but he good-naturedly prepared beds for all—a reasonably simple process in Vietnam, involving no more than throwing a straw mat down on the floor and turning on a fan. Within moments the upstairs room, with its enormous shrine to the ancestors taking up most of the space, was home to a half dozen or so snoring, drunken fishermen. All had been careful, naturally, to face their feet away from the shrine and each other's heads.

I woke up late in the hot morning. Curtains had been drawn against the sun, and Vu sat looking down at me with his hair wet. His naked chest was strong and burnt a dark brown, so that you could only just make out the black scorpions that danced across the smooth curves of his muscles. My head pounded. 'I was watching you while you slept,' he said gently, smiling at the memory. I shuddered at the vision—drunk, smelly, snoring like a trooper and doubtless dribbling, seeing me asleep must not have been a pleasant sight. 'You looked *so* beautiful,' he whispered, '*qua dep*—just like an angel.'

It happened that that day was *ram*, the Buddhist sabbath. Thao's older brother was the first to come around and tell me that, as an act of devotion, a car had been arranged to take us to the big Buddha at Phan Thiet. Naturally, I was paying for the car. We were all very, very hungover, and once we were all piled in the rented minibus the lingering smell of alcohol was obvious. But it was *ram*, and the fishermen all owed it to their mothers to make some kind of effort on this day.

For some reason the conversation turned to Tiger's masturbatory habits. Tiger was easily distinguished from the others by the tiny but striking tattoo he bore in the middle of his forehead—apparently an old but fading tradition among the fishermen of Mui Ne. It was Tiger's proud boast that he masturbated every day, and this was viewed by the others as a feat of enviable strength and courage. Vietnamese men are heavily influenced by the old Taoist superstitions that see semen as a finite product and its expulsion as enervating and damaging to the body. The other fishermen said they would only dare ejaculate once a week; one or two claimed to do it no more than once a month. It was universally agreed that the act itself left them exhausted and incapable of sustained activity.

Tiger laughed and said that he himself had done it that morning, just before we set out on our pleasure trip. 'No!' they said unbelieving. 'Hungover and committed to a full day out, you went and did it? You're a maniac! You'll collapse on the way. You've gotta stop this or you'll get old before your time.'

'Fellas!' cried the minibus driver. 'I'll remind you that it's *ram* and that we are headed to the pagoda. Is this any way for polite people to speak on such a day?' Suitably chastened, the fishermen fell silent, though when I turned back to look at him Tiger shot me an exaggerated, conspiratorial wink, his eyes twinkling with masculine pride.

The entrance to the big Buddha at Phan Thiet looks suspiciously like a tourist park, and my heart sank a little more as we drove through the gates. I was convinced that I was being sucked into a ghastly tourist trap, and my convictions only strengthened when I came face to face with a cable car. But the fishermen were in a frenzy of excited pleasure, almost skipping at the prospect of catching the cable car up the mountain. One was saying, 'I haven't been up there in years!' Another, 'My dear mother used to take me up once a year at *Vu Lan*, before she died, of course. Oh, how it makes me remember her.' So I gritted my teeth and bought the tickets for ten people.

The view from the cable car was a drag, but then vistas have always bored me. What fascinated me was the temple at the top of the mountain, a shoddy, patched-together kind of place that had been built for a community of nuns who had obviously started life as hermits.

The fishermen got busy with their own devotions, buying incense and bowing down before the various statues and shrines. Little trails led further up the mountain, so we followed those and arrived at a long, sun-filled terrace featuring giant statues of the Pure Land Buddhist Trinity—Amitabha flanked by Kwan Yin and Mahasthamaprapta Bodhisattva. They pointed to some little steps leading further up the mountain, and we trudged up those.

At the top was a truly exquisite sight: a vast reclining Buddha carved into the side of the mountain. White and stark and really quite beautiful, he shone in the hot sun. Pilgrims were everywhere on this sabbath day, and a contingent of rather fearsome nuns was patrolling the base of the Buddha, making sure people didn't do any of the things that were forbidden in a long list displayed at the Buddha's feet.

The first prohibition read: 'Do not climb or sit on the Glorious Buddha.' Glancing up, I saw Tiger scaling the Buddha's face, aiming for a perfect photograph sitting atop his head. A furious little nun ran over and began shouting at him to come down. He replied politely that he would be straight down, but not before he called out to one of the others to quickly take a couple of snaps. Later he said he'd have them blown up to poster size, as they would make fine souvenirs.

As we walked back down the mountain I heard the nuns at their prayers. I wanted to go back to the prayer hall and sit with the holy women while they chanted, to be washed over with their devotion. The tacky little temple was crowded to over-flowing, the nuns in neat rows at the front and the grey-robed laywomen in less organised formations at the back.

They started in on the Great Compassion Mantra of Kwan Yin, a twisting, complex series of sounds without literal mean-ing but filled with spiritual power. The women's eyes were closed, as each of them knew the long mantra by heart, and they were singing it with great force and feeling. This point of the liturgy was almost a frenzy, the monosyllables of the mantra being spoken faster and faster as the wooden drum picked up its beat. I felt lifted by the mantra, by the combined power of the women's voices. I was on my way home, now. The Great Compassion Mantra would surround me and be my protector all the way through. These sounds would stay in my mind, in my soul, forever, I was sure.

And then the great bell sounded and the women fell for-ward as one, their foreheads touching the floor in immense relief at the end of the mantra and also as an act of ultimate devotion to the Gentle Mother. There was complete silence and I awkwardly, hurriedly, fell forward too, feeling the cool of the tiles against my forehead. Hundreds of women surrounded me, and the fishermen sat outside waiting impatiently.

But for this one moment I was alone with the Goddess. I was moved, quite beyond expression, by the sense of uni-versal love. By the longing for it, if not its actual presence. This desire was embodied in the crowd around me, silent and singular too, dressed alike in their grey cotton robes; the bald, austere women at their head. This was a shared aspiration, and a quiet reassurance that the qualities of the Goddess—her all-encompassing embrace and monumental compassion—were present, not just in the room, but in our very selves. I was lost in this embrace, returned once more to the gentle arms of the mother.

IN POLICE CUSTODY
IN TRA VINH

Before I left Vietnam I was invited to the province of Tra Vinh, one of those unremarkable outposts to the south of Ho Chi Minh City that the Saigonese refer to as 'out west'. Tra Vinh is populated largely by people who are ethnically Khmer, and the television station there dedicates many of its broadcasts to that language. Lac, a tall, dark-skinned Khmer monk who lived in a desperately crowded monastery in the slums of Ho Chi Minh City, wanted me to come with him to his home town. He insisted that in these rarely visited areas the Khmer people still lead a traditional life—a way of life wiped out by Pol Pot within the borders of Cambodia itself.

The villages were, indeed, idyllic, and the smiling, beautiful Khmer with their strong bodies and sparkling eyes showed me unimaginable kindness. Lac's own family was rather extravagantly populated with nine brothers, and they made a fuss of both of us. Lac was the baby of the family, and poverty had forced him into the monastery for good while still a very small boy. Now in his twenties, the family all seemed to acknowledge his sacrifice and treated him with great reverence.

We stayed in the village monastery, a vast complex that was run like a chapter from *The Lord of the Flies*. In the Khmer tradition young men only serve in a monastery for a few years, and then they disrobe and marry. As a result, this beautiful and quite ancient religious institution was ruled and managed entirely by boys. The startlingly youthful abbott was a picture of good health, his biceps bulging from his robes as he tore apart a pomelo for my evening supper.

Staying in the village proved not to be easy, however. A heavy-handed local policeman came solemnly to the monastery after the first night and told the abbott that I was not permitted on the premises. I was whisked away to Lac's little family home, where the best bed was vacated for me and I spent an evening perspiring under a mosquito net with four of Lac's brothers, all determined to observe this exotic foreigner in every stage of his day. The next morning the same portly policeman turned up on their porch and told them I was forbidden goods. He was a policeman of the old school, authoritarian and petty, and insisted that the old rules still existed. Foreigners, he intoned, were not permitted to stay in private homes, and indeed were not permitted in Khmer areas at all.

I was transported in convoy to the local police station, which I noticed was in the grounds of a Buddhist nunnery. I sat for hours on a hard wooden bench while the local chief stared mournfully at my passport for long periods and sighed.

I attempted to be charming but these attempts at good cheer were met with rather severe glares. Lac was fetched from the monastery to negotiate my release, but it appeared that the policeman was a good Communist, and monks carried absolutely no influence with him. Lac suggested I pay him a bribe, but I refused the idea. My libertarian ire was being raised, and I insisted calls be placed to Saigon.

Eventually the over-zealous official spoke to someone in the city, and they duly informed him that I was at complete liberty to travel wherever I wanted and stay wherever I pleased in Vietnam. This information did not please him, however, and he insisted that I leave his district immediately. It was late in the day and all buses had stopped, a fact he was well aware of. A junior official was summoned and instructed to take me back to Tra Vinh city, a five- or six-hour drive. The young official solemnly nodded and my heart sank—I didn't fancy five back-breaking hours on the back of his motorcycle, with luggage.

Arriving at Lac's house to fetch my things, the young official smiled at me cheekily and said, in perfect English, 'Don't worry—tonight you can stay at my house. My brother is getting married!' And indeed he was. We rode to a rather palatial Vietnamese farmhouse, and a wedding party of the most elaborate kind was in full swing. My gatecrashing was viewed with great good cheer and, inevitably, some of Lac's rugged and voluble brothers were there, claiming me as an old family friend.

Like all Vietnamese celebrations, wedding parties can go on for quite an extended period, particularly in the country-side. The groom was drunk, a result of the constant rounds of toasting he had to oversee, travelling from table to table with a bottle of home-distilled rice vodka and a thick little glass. He was dressed preposterously in a white double-breasted suit and a red satin shirt. He was sweating profusely and the shirt was unbuttoned almost to the waist, exposing a substantial golden dragon pendant. When he saw me, he pointed to the pendant and then to himself. 'Me, I am dragon too,' he slurred, and his brother explained that his name was Dragon.

I was squeezed in at the table of honour, despite my slightly down-at-heel appearance, fresh from my incarceration. Now every second toast was directed at me, and Dragon, the groom, frequently leant down and wrapped me in a long, sweaty and alcohol-scented embrace. 'What good fortune!' he would cry. 'How auspicious! Oh, I will have fine fat sons now that this man has visited my wedding.'

As the night wore on I began to fade somewhat, but the newly married Dragon was keen to keep partying. He pulled up a little plastic stool and sat by me, waxing lyrical about his happiness. Then he said, 'Tonight is my special night. I want to share it with you. I will take you on a tour.' Despite the protests of his mother and the bride herself Dragon went looking for his motorcycle keys, and soon we were tearing down the dirt lanes of a nameless Khmer village in the back blocks of Tra Vinh province. The driver was dangerously drunk and his passenger was a fugitive, but it was a full-moon night and the light shone beautifully off the big temples and the orchards of pomelo trees.

I didn't know where we were going and, anyhow, I half-expected to die at any moment, so erratically were we swaying down ever-diminishing tracks. At last we came to a halt. It was late, and Dragon tore off his wedding jacket and then his red satin shirt. The golden pendant glinted on his muscled chest. 'Look around you, Big Brother,' he whispered. We were in a clearing, but we were not alone. All around us were the silhouettes of ruined walls and towers. An elaborate, Cambodian-style roof was silhouetted against the moon, though underneath it there was nothing but grass. It was the remains of an old temple complex, entirely abandoned and quite unnerving.

Dragon strolled about the ruins, his torso sweaty in the hot night. 'There are ghosts here,' he said solemnly. 'This was a big temple, destroyed in the war. Many boys died here, and now at night you can hear them at their prayers.'

We both stopped, and in the breeze and echo of the cicadas I could hear them, their adolescent voices breaking as they struggled with their clumsy chanting. The ghosts of poor dead boys chanting forever, hoping to return home to their mothers and sweethearts at the end of their period of celibacy. Perhaps Dragon's own brothers were among the ghosts, certainly cousins and family friends.

Dragon had been celebrating, drunk and showing off on the happiest night of his life. Soon we would return to the party and he would be with his beautiful new wife. Soon enough I too would return to my own home thousands of kilometres away, to my own comforts and conveniences.

But in the moonlight we stood in the bombed-out temple, and history and tragedy pressed in on us on every side. And all we could hear were the ghostly prayers of the young men who could never, ever go home.

HOMEWARD
BOUND

Normally, before I leave a place, I am overcome with exhaustion and inertia. The act of leaving is, perhaps, too emotional for me. I disgrace myself by not saying proper goodbyes, not going to see people one last time. I am vague in discussing the exact time and date I will be leaving, not wanting people to come to the airport and see me off.

When I came to Vietnam I was confused about my beliefs, determined to get them straightened, solidified. But my time there had only further infected me with that sliding approach to religious affiliation that is so common in Asia. The necessity to define, to identify as one thing, is not apparent, or even useful, in Vietnam. I was exactly as I was when I arrived, a passionate devotionalist, a believer in spiritual potential and a lover of most paths to the transcendent.

In Vietnam I didn't really have to explain what I was, largely because people already had a fantasy about what I represented. They had imagined a position for me, and I was free to roam at will around their assumptions.

When I was at Tan Son Nhat airport waiting to come home, a large family came into the waiting lounge. The lounge was almost entirely empty—as usual, I had been one of the first to check in. The family then proceeded to sit all around me, in front of me and behind me. They chatted to one another noisily, passing around snacks and bottles of liniment, seemingly unaware of my presence there directly in the middle of them all. There must have been a hundred empty seats in that empty lounge; perhaps they had felt sorry for me, sitting there all alone.

Throughout my trip I had noticed this sensitivity to the lonely, this desire to alleviate someone's sorrow by being with them, by acknowledging their presence even if you were never going to engage them. When I stayed in monasteries the monks couldn't bear the thought of me being left alone, and envoys were despatched to sit with me and keep me happy, though I craved solitude.

For me, travel is a lonely business. I often think that foreign travel, like a foreign film, is best enjoyed on one's own. But in Vietnam solitude is nigh on impossible. It is a culture based on companionship, on the comforts of family and community. To be alone is the ultimate in sadness.

Even the spirits and the wandering, hungry ghosts of Vietnam are never allowed to suffer in solitude. Most people are scrupulous in making offerings to these poor lost souls, people who have no family to remember them. Perhaps due to many generations of shared suffering, the Vietnamese like to observe a shared remembering, one that includes the lonely and wandering of all realms—even foreign tourists.

Just before I was due to leave, the strap on my luggage broke. It was an aggravation; it meant that on my last day I would have to trudge around Ho Chi Minh City and try to buy a new bag. But Kien, my great friend and rescuer, who had taken an entire day off work to help me with my packing and to revel in an orgy of sadness at my leaving, remonstrated with me for my wasteful ways. He jumped on his motorcycle with the broken bag and was back within a half hour, the bag repaired and probably ready now for a hundred more journeys. Nothing is thrown away in Vietnam, where recycling is a necessity rather than an ideological position.

I had left home in a great deal of excitement, too much so. My life was heading in a hundred different directions at once, and I felt exhausted just thinking of the various roads I would have to take, all at the same time. But three months in Vietnam, with its inconveniences and discomforts, its frustrations and exploitations, its infuriating multiplicity—it had somehow calmed me. I had found a resolve, an inner strength that I knew would stand me in good stead for the time to come.

I had been patched up, in a rough and tumble way, and was ready now for a hundred more journeys.

BIBLIOGRAPHY

Acton, Harold (1984) *Memoirs of a Aesthete*, London: Hamish Hamilton

Adler, Laure (1998) *Marguerite Duras: A Life*, London: Phoenix

Anonymous (2008) *The Discourse on the Ten Wholesome Ways of Action and a Lecture of the Excellent Karma Resulting from the Practice of the Ten Commandments*, Taipei: The Corporate Body of the Buddha Educational Foundation

Anonymous (n.d.) 'The New Canonical Codes/ *Tan Luat*', http://www.personal.usyd.edu.au/~cdao/tanluat.htm (accessed 8/5/09)

Anonymous (2008) *The Sutra of Buddha's Bequeathed Teachings, The Enlightenment Sutra with Annotations, The Sutra of Forty-Two Sections*, Taipei: The Corporate Body of the Buddha Educational Foundation

Asma, Stephen T. (2005) *The Gods Drink Whiskey*, San Francisco: Harper San Francisco

Bernstein, Richard (2001) *Ultimate Journey*, New York: Vintage

Borchert, Thomas (2007) 'Buddhism, Politics and Nationalism in the Twentieth and Twenty-first Centuries', *Religion Compass* 1:5 pp. 529–546

Boucher, Sandy (1999) *Discovering Kwan Yin*, Boston: Beacon Press

Burkhardt, V. R. (1982) *Chinese Creeds and Customs*, Hong Kong: South China Morning Post

Chang, Hui-Ching (1997) 'Language and Words: Communication in the *Analects* of Confucius', *Journal of Language and Social Psychology* 16:2 pp. 107–131

Cleary, J. C. (2000) 'Introduction to Pure Land Buddhism' in Suddhisuka (ed.) *Taming the Monkey Mind*, Taipei: The Corporate Body of the Buddha Educational Foundation, pp. 91–106

Conze, Edward (1959) *Buddhism: Its Essence and Development*, New York: Harper Torchbooks

Cooke, Nola (2008) 'Strange Brew: Global, Regional and Local Factors Behind the Prohibition of Christian Practices in Nguyen Cochinchina', *Journal of Southeast Asian Studies* 39:3 pp. 383–410

Crow, David (2000) *In Search of the Medicine Buddha*, New York: Jeremy P. Tarcher

Dessaix, Robert (2008) *Arabesques*, Sydney: Picador

Dowrick, Stephanie (2009) 'Reading the Signals', *Good Weekend* 9 May, p. 53

Duras, Marguerite (1986) *The Lover*, London: Flamingo

Elliott, Duong Van Mai (1999) *The Sacred Willow*, Oxford: Oxford University Press

FitzGerald, Frances (1972) *Fire in the Lake*, Boston: Atlantic–Little, Brown

FitzGerald, Frances and Cross, Mary (2001) *Vietnam: Spirits of the Earth*, Boston: Bulfinch Press

Fowler, Jeaneane D. (2005) *An Introduction to the Philosophy and Religion of Taoism: Pathways to Immortality*, Sussex: Sussex Academic Press

Hartingh, Bertrand de et al (2007) *Vietnam Style*, Singapore: Periplus Editions

Haslip, Le Ly (1989) *When Heaven and Earth Changed Places*, London: Pan Books

Hickey, Gerald Cannon (1964) *Village in Vietnam*, New Haven: Yale University Press

Hoang Dang Bui and Hum Dac Bui (n.d.) 'The Collection of Divine Messages/ *Thanh Ngon Hiep Tuyen* Vol. 1', http://www.personal.usyd.edu.au/~cdao/tnht1e1.htm (accessed 8/5/09)

Huy, Nguyen Van and Kendall, Laurel (2003) *Vietnam: Journeys of Body, Mind, and Spirit*, Berkeley: University of California Press

Jones, Tobias (2007) *Utopian Dreams*, London: Faber & Faber

Kiang, Koh Kok and Yee, Patrick (2004) *Guan Yin: Goddess of Compassion*, Singapore: Asiapac

Kolko, Gabriel (1987) *Vietnam: Anatomy of War 1940–1975*, London: Unwin Paperbacks

Luk, Charles (2001) *The Surangama Sutra*, New Delhi: Munshiram Manoharlal

McCarthy, Patrician (2007) *The Face Reader*, New York: Penguin

McHale, Shawn Frederick (2004) *Print and Power: Confucianism, Communism and Buddhism in the Making of Modern Vietnam*, Honolulu: University of Hawaii Press

Ma Van Khang (2000) *Against the Flood*, Willimantic: Curbstone Press

Nguyen Duy Hinh (2007) 'Religious Life in Vietnamese History', *Nghien Cuu Ton Giao* (Religious Studies Review) 1:3 pp. 3–13

O'Reilley, Mary Rose (2000) *The Barn at the End of the World*, Minneapolis: Milkweed Editions

Phan Boi Chau (Vinh Sinh and Nicholas Wickenden tr.) (1999) *Overturned Chariot: The Autobiography of Phan Boi Chau*, Honolulu: University of Hawaii Press

Poncins, Gontran De (1957) *From a Chinese City*, Palo Alto: Trackless Sands Press

Proschan, Frank (2002) 'Eunuch Mandarins, *Soldats Mamzelles*, Effeminate Boys and Graceless Women: French Colonial Constructions of Vietnamese Genders', *GLQ* 8:4 pp. 435–467

Proschan, Frank (2002) '"Syphilis, Opiomania and Pederasty": Colonial Constructions of Vietnamese (and French) Social Diseases', *Journal of the History of Sexuality* 11:4 pp. 610–636

Raso, Jack (1993) *Mystical Diets*, Buffalo: Prometheus Books

Saran, Mishi (2005) *Chasing the Monk's Shadow*, New Delhi: Penguin

Schneider, David (2008) 'Sacred Seeds', *Tricycle* xvii:3 pp. 56–59

Shah, Tahir (2002) *In Search of King Solomon's Mines*, London: John Murray

Shih-Hsien Hsing-An Chan Master (2003) *A Composition Urging the Generation of the Bodhi Mind*, Taipei: The Corporate Body of the Buddha Educational Foundation

Stevens, Keith (1997) *Chinese Gods*, London: Collins & Brown

Theroux, Paul (2008) *Ghost Train to the Eastern Star*, Melbourne: Penguin

Thich Nhat Hanh (1988) *The Heart of Understanding*, Berkeley: Parallax Press

Thich Nhat Hanh (1997) *Stepping Into Freedom*, Berkeley: Parallax Press

Thich Thien An (1970) *Zen Buddhism and Nationalism in Vietnam*, Los Angeles: International Buddhist Meditation Center

Thich Thien Tam (1992) *Pure Land Buddhism*, Sepulveda: International Buddhist Monastic Institute

Tri Hai Bhikkhuni (n.d.) *Buddhism in Vietnam: Past and Present* (booklet printed in Vietnam, late 1990s)

Unger, Ann Helen and Walter (1997) *Pagodas, Gods and Spirits of Vietnam*, London: Thames & Hudson

Versfeld, Martin (2005) *The Philosopher's Cookbook*, Sydney: Figment Publishing

Wright, Gwendolyn (1991) *The Politics of Design in French Colonial Urbanism*, Chicago: University of Chicago Press

Wu Cheng-En (1961) *Monkey*, Middlesex: Penguin

Yin Kuang (Thich Thien Tam tr.) (1997) *Pure-Land Zen, Zen Pure Land*, New York: Sutra Translation Committee of the United States and Canada

Yutang, Lin (1938) *The Wisdom of Confucius*, New York: The Modern Library